THE ENGLISH RELIGIOUS DRAMA

THE

ENGLISH RELIGIOUS DRAMA

BY

KATHARINE LEE BATES

KENNIKAT PRESS, INC./PORT WASHINGTON, N. Y.

THE ENGLISH RELIGIOUS DRAMA

Originally published in 1893
Reissued in 1966 by Kennikat Press

Library of Congress Catalog Card No: 65-18602

CONTENTS.

CHAPTER I.

PAGE

LATIN PASSION PLAYS AND SAINT PLAYS . . . 1

CHAPTER II.

MIRACLE PLAYS — DESCRIPTION 35

CHAPTER III.

MIRACLE PLAYS — ENUMERATION 88

CHAPTER IV.

MIRACLE PLAYS — DRAMATIC VALUES 168

CHAPTER V.

MORALITIES 201

APPENDIX.

TOPICAL OUTLINE AND REFERENCES · . . . 240

THE ENGLISH RELIGIOUS DRAMA

CHAPTER I.

PASSION PLAYS AND SAINT PLAYS.

THE history of the European theatre, not only
west of the Channel, but upon the Continent as
well, bears resemblance to the history of the little
English robin, who, as his strength waxes and his
breast brightens and his song grows tuneful, turns
his ungrateful bill against the parents who have
reared him, so that the misty autumn mornings ring
with melodious defiances and cries of combat between the young birds and the old. In like manner
the romantic drama, born of the Church and nour-
ished by the Church, came in time, as it acquired
an independent life and gradually passed from sacred
to secular uses, to incur the resentful hostility of
the parent bird, whose plumage its mischievous
young activity loved to ruffle.

It is not only the Christian drama which has a
religious basis. We find religious passion at the
heart of the drama of ancient India and of modern

Persia, while the very name tragedy confesses the
outgrowth of the Attic stage from sacrificial ceremonies.   At the altar of Dionysus, giver of wine,
giver of joy, giver of freedom, while the goat, the
thank-offering, stood waiting to be slain, the shaggy-
vestured priests, with one wild rhythm of voice
and step and gesture, chanted an anthem of praise
known as the goat-song (τράγος ᾠδή), or tragedy.
So the pæon, with music of the flutes and rhythmic
dancing, was sung at Delphi in honour of Apollo ;
and song, too, entered into the mystic worship of
Demeter at Eleusis.   And as at Delphi there grew
up, in connection with the lyric service, a representation of the victory of the young god of light
over the deadly serpent, and as at Eleusis the rape
of Persephone and the wanderings of Demeter,
shown by the uncertain light of torches, were
woven into the symbolical rites, so from the choral
worship of Dionysus, by slower and more even
steps, leading to transcendent height, rose the
classic drama.

Yet even in beauty-loving Hellas there was a sentiment opposed to theatrical representation.   Solon
is reported to have said, on meeting the car of
Thespis, that somewhat dim-featured founder of
Greek tragedy: "Are you not ashamed to tell so
many lies?"   And the man of truth, Lycurgus,
would allow no theatre in Sparta.

It was at Rome, however, in the early centuries of Christianity, that the cry against the drama waxed loud, and not without reason; for the Roman stage was, from the outset, dull, trifling, vulgar, and grew to be brutal, foul, horrible. The most celebrated of Latin playwrights, Plautus and Terence, belonged to the lowest ranks of society, for the followers of the art so honoured and beloved in republican Athens were disdained at republican Rome, and even under the Empire not all the golden patronage of a Nero or a Domitian could eradicate from Romans of the good old stock their prejudice against the histrionic craft. An actor who accepted payment forfeited thereby his rights of citizenship. The scorn of the Roman state was based, however, on grounds less worthy than those whereon rested in these later times the disapproval of the Christian Church. Again and again she urged her members to refrain from attending the theatre, threatening to cast forth from her communion those who persisted in this amusement. Actors she would not receive save on condition of relinquishment of their profession. There was a striking case of the actor Genesius, who, being baptised on the stage in mimicry of the Christian sacrament, was so impressed by the solemn ceremony that henceforth he held himself christened in very truth, sealed his profession with his blood in Diocletian's persecution, and was enrolled by the Church upon her list of saints.

But still in the fourth century, and even in the fifth, we find the Church warning, rebuking, excommunicating, her theatre-goers. St. Augustine, in his wild youth at Carthage, dearly loved a play. This taste, repented later, was destined to rise against him in whimsical form enough, when, centuries after he had been laid to rest in bishop's vestments, he appeared on the mediæval miracle stage as a didactic master of ceremonies. But the Church, although her prohibitions and penances, her denunciations and excommunications, together with the tide of tumultuous times and the working of inherent decay, finally swept the ancient drama from the boards, had resorted meanwhile to subtler means for weaning her children from these pagan plays.

As early as the close of the second century, a Scriptural tragedy, founded upon Exodus and having for its chief characters Moses, Sapphora, and God from the Bush, had been written by a Jew named Ezekiel. In the fourth century Apollinarius the Elder, a priest of Laodicea, rewrote parts of the Old Testament history in Homeric hexameters, and worked over other parts into dramatic form, while Bishop Apollinarius, his son, recast the New Testament into Platonic dialogues. A curious drama entitled Χριστὸς Πάσχων — Christ's Passion — has been long believed to be from the pen of St. Gregory Nazianzene, Patriarch of Constantinople in the latter part of the fourth century. The play is cast in the Attic mould, hymns of the Church being substituted for the original choruses. The action takes place behind the scenes and is announced by messengers, usually by the Virgin Mary. There are a few verses from Æschylus, chiefly from the *Prometheus Bound*, and from Euripides is borrowed a third of the entire verse of the play, including Mary's lament for the crucified Christ, which is identical with Agavè's lament for her son in the *Bacchanals*. This portion of the loan was not returned to the owner; for the lamentation, having been applied to a use so sacred, was afterwards omitted by the monastic copyists from all texts of Euripides. It has been held that this composite production found its way from Constantinople into Italy, thence becoming known to western Europe and suggesting to the mediæval clergy the expedient of impressing the Scripture story upon their rude audiences by spectacular representation; but the latest editor of the Χριστὸς Πάσχων, Dr. Brambs (Leipzig, 1885), has confounded these excellent theories by deciding, from a searching investigation of the metre, prosody, and grammar of the play, that it can by no means be attributed to St. Gregory, but belongs some six hundred years later. Classic imitations somewhat similar to Χριστὸς

Πάσχων appeared in these later times, but in the Latin tongue and with the stamp upon them of Latin drama rather than of Greek.

For the tenth century, dark as it was, — the "starless century" so-called, — occasionally witnessed within Benedictine cloisters the acting of dramatised legends of the saints, these being written in the Roman manner. Their best remembered author is a German nun, Hroswitha, of Gandersheim in Saxony, she who was styled "the Christian Sappho" and "the loud voice from Gandersheim," and who, turning the unholy leaves of Terence with one hand, while she kept the other on her beads, assimilated so much of his style and phraseology as to enable her to produce a few comedies after the external likeness of his own. Her themes, far different from those of her model, are martyrdom and the glorification of chastity. But we are not to conclude, from the appearance in the long mediæval period of an occasional Greek or Latin play, written from an open Euripides or Terence, by a priest here or a nun there, acted within the cloisters and before the limited audiences of the learned, that in these we find the fountain-head of the European theatre. Great movements do not spring from origins of such a forced and conscious character. Ward is the first of English critics to clearly point out that the Passion Play, in which the modern drama takes its rise, itself sprang from the liturgical service of the Roman Church. It is but the history of the Attic stage repeated. Ward discovers in the mystical liturgy of the Mass, with its blending of symbolic action, Scriptural narrative, and outbursts of song, an artistic conception, a dramatic progression, with pantomimic, epical, and lyrical elements. He notes that, as early as the fifth century, this service, itself so picturesque and impressive, and, in those early days, still elastic, not bound fast, as now, to a fixed ritual, was embellished, on high church festivals, as Easter and Christmas, by the addition of living tableaux to illustrate the gospel story. These tableaux would naturally come to be accompanied by antiphonal singing, with a growing effect of question and answer, while gesture and action would gradually be introduced. Indeed, the service of the Church being in Latin, there was from a very early period especial appeal to the eye. In Germany, at least, the priest was wont, in reading the gospel story, to slowly unfold a roll which, on the side toward the congregation, was pictured over with the figures and scenes forming the subjects of the text. Church paintings, carvings, statues, bas-reliefs, altar pieces, emblazoned windows, crucifixes, were all further and more elaborate attempts at an ocular translation of the Latin gospels for the curious, longing, unlettered people. The tableaux vivants were but another step in the same direction, action another, while the breaking up the Scripture text into dialogue and the gradual addition and substitution of vernacular phrases were the inevitable sequences of these.

The three great days of the Christian year, Christmas, Good Friday, and Easter, gave chief occasion for these graphic and elaborate services. We should need to become as little children and enter into the hearts of the French and Italian babies of to-day, as lifted high in a mother's arms, or on a father's shoulder, to view the mimic Bethlehem in candle-lighted chapel, they throw delighted kisses to golden-haired Mary and white-bearded Joseph, to the glittering star, and to the smiling Christ-Child, if we would realise what these representations signified in the religious development of a mediæval congregation. That most engaging of saints, Francis of Assisi, built a Christmas manger in the woods, and pictured the beautiful group of the Nativity by means of living men and women, with a genuine baby, and a genuine ox and ass. Yet our own exchange of Christmas gifts should do something toward bringing us into sympathy with the days when the peasants of Flanders used to lay at the feet of the Christ-Child their shepherd-offerings of eggs and cheese, while the great and noble brought precious tribute, as representing the Magi of the East.

The primitive Passion drama was nothing more than the solemn lowering the crucifix on Good Friday, the laying it away beneath the altar, and the raising it again, with anthems of rejoicing, on the Resurrection festival. Mr. Pollard has pointed out that a trace of the old observance yet lingers in the custom of veiling the crucifix from Holy Thursday to the first evensong of Easter. But the hollowed place beneath the altar did not long suffice, as the ritual became more and more magnificent, for the reception of the crucifix or of the gilded picture, or carven figure, sometimes substituted in this ceremony for the crucifix. Temporary sepulchres of wood were built in arched recesses of the chancel wall, on the north, and by the fourteenth century these in turn gave way, in many churches both of England and the Continent, to permanent structures of stone. An interesting record remains of Durham : —

"Within the church of Durham, upon Good Friday, there was a marvellous solemn service, in which service time, after the Passion was sung, two of the eldest monks took a goodly large crucifix all of gold of the semblance of our Saviour Christ, nailed upon the Cross. . . . The service being ended, the said two monks carried the Cross to the Sepulchre with great reverence (which Sepulchre was set up that morning on the north side of the choir, nigh unto the High Altar, before the service time) and there did lay it within the said Sepulchre with great devotion."

Upon these sepulchres was lavished rich beauty of carving and of colour. The sleeping soldiers, their weapons drooping in their hands, were carved upon the lower portion, and upon the upper the hovering figures of attendant angels. The sepulchre was guarded during the night preceding Easter Sunday by some officer of the church, who was duly paid for his vigil. So late as 1558, the "accompts" of St. Helen's, Abingdon, contain the following items : —

"Payde for making the sepulture, 10s."

"For peynting the same sepulture, 3s."

"For stones, and other charges about it, 4s. 6d."

"To the sexton for meat and drink, and watching the sepulture, according to custom, 22d."

The black-robed bier that stands in the choir of Roman churches during Lent, with the mournful ritual of Good Friday, and such permanent church decorations as the artificial mound at Antwerp, a miniature Calvary crowned with its three crucifixes, help us understand how the early Passion Plays were fostered. Still in the chapel of the Vatican, on Good Friday, after the reading of the Old Testament prophecies, the Passion from the Gospel of John is sung with voices disposed as in an oratorio, the tenor taking the part of Christ, the bass of Pilate, while choruses of the priests, of the soldiers, of the people, are interspersed with the evangelical narrative in recitative.

Roman missals of the present day still retain the following dramatic colloquy, which, originally sung

with appropriate action by two choirmen representing SS. Peter and John and by three others personating the three Marys, is now rendered musically,
without action, by the basses and trebles.

Apostoli. Dic nobis, Maria,
   Quid vidisti in via.

Prima Maria. Sepulchrum Christi viventis
   Et gloriam resurgentis.

Secunda Maria. Angelicos testes
   Sudarium et vestes.

Tertia Maria. Surrexit Christus spes mea,
   Præcedit vos in Galilæam.

Apostoli. Credendum est magis soli ⎫ Omitted in
   Mariæ veraci   ⎪ modern missals.
   Quam Judæorum   ⎬ Found in old
   Pravæ cohorti.   ⎭ York missal.

Omnes. Scimus Christum surrexisse
   A mortuis vere.
   Tu nobis, victor Rex, miserere.

The old liturgical dramas, played in the churches,
with priests for actors and worshippers for audience,
were slow to break away from their intimate connection with the service. Even in the thirteenth
century and in the case of a somewhat elaborate
Good Friday drama, written partly in Latin and
partly in the German vernacular, the play appears
to be still blended with the liturgy, one stage direction enjoining upon the Virgin that she, after concluding her chant of lamentation over the crucified

Christ, should sit down quietly, for an hour, and then arise and play again. No part of the play was going on meanwhile, and it would obviously have been an appropriate period for continuing the service, invested, from the recent representation of the Passion, with peculiar solemnity.

If we would look upon one of these primitive dramas, so unconscious of its own dramatic nature and dramatic destiny, we must thread our way through blossomed English lanes and enter the grateful cool of the high-arched cathedral. About us is a motley multitude, — nobles in scarlet hose and tunics of cloth of gold, ladies in bright-hued trailing gowns with floating sleeves and richly embroidered girdles, rainbow-vested children pattering along in blue and yellow shoes, as if stained from their treading among the violets and prim-roses, and peasant groups in coarser stuffs of ruder shape and duller tint. Yet there is colour every-where, the raiment of the worshippers almost seem-ing to catch the broken lights from the great windows that gleam like marvellous jewels east and west and forth from shadowy aisles. And the well-wrought stone of capital and canopy and crocket has tints of russet and of buff, and the walls are fairly frescoed, and statues, coloured to the look of life, repose on the gem-set tombs of bishops and of princes. It is an age of art, an era of perception and of feeling. The trooping multitude brings eyes and ears all sensitive and eager. The very influences of the sacred place quicken the æsthetic craving. These mediæval church-goers, even the meagre and the ragged, long for a service vivid, exquisite, aglow with life and beauty. But the scientific and philosophic faculties are not yet hungry. The mental world of these thought-children is peopled by angels, saints, and devils in company with ghosts, fairies, and hobgoblins. Of these the devil is undoubtedly the favourite, calling out half-terrified interest and half-triumphant respect. It is the devil who figures most conspicuously in carving and in speech. Perhaps in this very Easter congregation kneels the haughty dame whose sweeping robe called out the satire of a bitter-tongued old monk : —

"I have heard of a proud woman," he says, "who wore a white dress with a long train, which, trailing behind her, raised a dust even as far as the altar and the crucifix. But as she left the church, and lifted up her train on account of the dirt, a certain holy man saw a devil laughing : and having adjured him to tell why he laughed, the devil said, 'A companion of mine was just now sitting on the train of that woman, using it as if it were his chariot, but when she lifted her train up, my companion was shaken off into the dirt ; and that is why I was laughing.'"

After the mental coma produced by the shock of

the barbaric invasion, after the blank of the Dark Ages, Europe, leaving science in the main to the Arabians, was content for a few centuries to busy herself in re-sharpening her dulled intellects on that curious, ingenious, ever-turning, and never-arriving grindstone, scholastic philosophy. The work was slowly and thoroughly done, wit waxed keen again, and when the passion for truth re-awakened, the instrument was ready. But meanwhile sensation, not reason, ruled high and low alike. Rich and poor pressed side by side to gaze upon the pigeon plume that was exhibited as a veritable feather of the Holy Ghost. Wounds were treated by anointing the swords that had inflicted them. Every superstition and every folly had almost unrestricted sway. Illiterate, illogical, — out of this mediæval Europe what good may come? The Gothic cathedral came, and in its heart the nascent Gothic drama.

But we were proposing to attend the Easter service with the gayly attired worshippers in this stately English minster. White-robed monks fill the dim, mysterious choir, the altar is heavily draped with black, the golden crucifix, thick set with jewels, is missing from its place, but on the north of the chancel we see the Easter sepulchre with the stone rolled away from the door. The solemn ritual of the Mass proceeds in wonted fashion, with fragrance of incense, with silver sound of bell, with kneelings and uprisings, with processional pomp and awful adoration, and over all the glory of the chant. But when, after a preparatory chorus of the prophets answered by a chorus of the church, there is reached that point in the service whereat the tender story of the Marys coming to the sepulchre was of old time rendered as an anthem, three choristers in long white stoles, bearing perfume-breathing censers, step forth from the singing band and walk slowly, with groping motions and dirge-like music, toward the north of the chancel. As they near the tomb, with gesture of surprise to see the open door, other white-raimented figures, with palm-branches in hand, rise from the mouth of the sepulchre to meet them, singing in sweet, high notes : —

"Quem quæritis in sepulchro, O Christicolæ ?"

The Marys make answer in softer, tremulous tone : —

"Jesum Nazarenum crucifixum, O cœlicolæ !"

And the angels respond with victorious cadence : —

"Non est hic, surrexit sicut prædixerat ;
Ite, nuntiate quia surrexit de sepulchro."

In obedience to the gesture of the angels, the Marys stoop to the opening of the tomb, draw forth the linen wrappings, and lifting these in sight of all the people, in token of that garment of death which the risen Christ has put off from him, turn to the chorus with exultant song : —

"Dominus surrexit de sepulchro !   Alleluia ! "

Then the Te Deum, rolling forth from all that multitude in impetuous thanksgiving, floods choir, nave, and transepts, the worshippers clasp one another, with tears raining down their faces, the black draperies are borne away, the altar glistens again in gold and rich embroidery, the shining crucifix is lifted to its place, and, simple as the representation has been, even the little lad in primrose shoes will never forget the service, nor the thrill of Easter joy in his own soul.

There are a few selfish moments, in which the people press tumultuously toward the carven choir-screen, in the belief that eyes which may behold the Easter elevation of the crucifix shall not close in death for the year to come ; but, as the tide ebbs, and the throng pours out into the sunshine, the living picture has done for them what no dogma, no argument, no philosophic analysis, would have had the power to do, and in devout rejoicing, neighbour greets neighbour with the sacred words, "The Lord is risen ! "

From brief dramatic actions, so blended with the service, there soon arose more extended and more elaborate Latin plays, that were represented, often quite by themselves, in the churches, on the appropriate festivals. The music of the former was merely that of the liturgical chant, save that special melodies were necessarily added where the dialogue exceeded the limits of the liturgical text. The latter had music composed expressly for them, even for those parts of the text included in the liturgy; and various stringed instruments were introduced to supplement the organ. The words set for God were sometimes rendered by three voices, — tenor, bass, and alto, — to signify the threefold nature. The old Latin hymns, many of them so luxuriously soft and mellifluous, so rich in sensuous imagery, played a leading part in these primitive oratorios.

The literary antiquities of England are not so fortunate as to include any specimens of the Latin liturgical drama; but one has survived in Holland, thirteen in Germany, and fourteen in France. From the French collection I paraphrase one of the simplest, a Christmas play, whose manuscript, gayly written in red and blue and brown, dates from the end of the thirteenth century, It is entitled

THE SHEPHERDS.

On the holy Christmas Eve, after the Te Deum, let the angel take his place, announce that Christ is born, and utter these words : —

"Fear not; for, behold, I bring you good tidings of great joy, which shall be to all people. For unto you is born this day in the city of David a Saviour. And this shall be a sign unto you, — ye shall find the babe wrapped in swaddling-clothes, lying in a manger."

Here let seven choir-boys, standing in the gallery above, chant : —

"Glory to God in the highest, and on earth peace, goodwill to men."

On hearing the song, let the shepherds move toward the manger, singing this response : —

> "Glory in the highest !
>   Peace to the human race !
>   Earth is linked to Heaven
>   By reconciling grace !
>
> "God the reconciler
>   Bows to human ban,
>   That into the gates of Paradise
>   May enter sinful man !
>   Alleluia !   Alleluia !
>
> "Let us go and see if so
>   The very God hath willed.
>   Let us go, that we may know
>   If the promise be fulfilled.
>
> "A baby cries in Bethlehem
>   Beneath the starry night.
>   The ancient adversary hears
>   And quakes for deadly fright.

" Let us come, oh, let us come
Where the Lord of all
With maiden mother makes his home
In an ox's stall."

Then let the shepherds, carrying crooks in their hands, walk through the midst of the choristers, close up to the Bethlehem, chanting as they go : —

" Let us now go even unto Bethlehem, and see this thing which is come to pass, which the Lord hath made known unto us."

As they draw near, two choristers, being in the stall as nursing-women, shall chant : —

" Tell, O shepherds, whom seek ye in the manger."

Let the shepherds make answer : —

" Christ the Lord and Saviour, a child wrapt in swaddling-clothes, even as the angel said."

Thereat the nursing-women, drawing aside a curtain, shall reveal the child, chanting in their turn : —

" Behold the little one with Mary his mother ! Behold him of whom long since the prophet Isaiah did tell ! "

Here let the chorus of choir-boys point out the mother, chanting : —

" Behold, a virgin shall conceive and shall bear a son ; but go ye and announce that the Christ is born."

Then should the shepherds bow themselves before
the Virgin, singing thus : —

> " Hail, O hail, all peerless maiden !
> Thine enclasping arm is laden
> With a child whose ages number
>   God's eternity.
> Let us worship him in slumber
>   On his mother's knee.
>
> " Mary, by thy mediation
> Grant our sinful souls salvation !
> Though as wheat the devil sift us,
>   Hold us in thy sight,
> That thy son at last may lift us
>   To his blessèd light ! "

And now that the child is clearly shown, let the
shepherds bow themselves before him ; then let them
turn to the chorus, chanting : —

"Alleluia ! Alleluia ! Now we know for a surety that
upon earth is born the Christ, in whose praise sing ye all
with the prophets, saying : "

And here, at once, let the Mass be begun, and
let the shepherds lead the choir, and chant the
Gloria in Excelsis.

While the Passion Play was thus generated in
the very heart of the holy service, the church processions were unconsciously working with the Passion
Play to produce what may best be designated as

Saint Plays. The summer festival of Corpus Christi, a feast founded by Pope Urban IV., in honour of the Sacred Host, in 1264, and universally accepted by 1311, was primarily a day of magnificent church parades, which contributed generously to the development of the religious drama. For it was not enough to carry in these processions images of the Virgin and pictures of the saints, but living copies of the holy personages, often gorgeously attired, and always bearing some explanatory emblem, — St. Andrew, his cross, the angel Gabriel, a lily, — walked in the midst, and received due homage from the gazing throngs. Here Adam and Eve would pass, lifting between them the Tree of Knowledge; and here John the Baptist leading a lamb; there St. George on his war-horse, trailing after him the green-scaled, gilt-hoofed body of the slain Dragon; or red-bearded Judas, bending beneath the weight of his money-bag, and closely followed by the horned and blackened Devil, considerately bringing along the gallows.

In France, the Corpus Christi pageants, which were very elaborate, never yielded to the spoken drama, but this one feast was kept sacred to procession and dumb show. In Merrie England, Corpus Christi failed to maintain to the end its purely processional character, but there was no lack of dramatic pageantry. The months of the year were counted off by the half-pagan, half-Christian ceremonies of the

successive holidays, — hawks and hounds at Michael-
mas, tricksy jests at Hallowe'en, feasting at Harvest
Home, Yuletide revels under the sway of the jolly
Lord of Misrule, bear-baiting and cock-fighting on
Shrove Tuesday, Robin Hood shows on Mayday, and
on the Eve of St. John the Baptist bonfires, torches,
and cressets, and the setting of the Midsummer
Watch. Even the palate helped keep track of the
seasons by the Easter buns and the Whitsuntide
roast lamb, the Christmas plum-pudding, and the New
Year wassail bowl. And very charmingly were the
changes of the sun marked by the sylvan adornments
of the house.

> "Down with the rosemary and bayes,
>   Down with the mistletoe ;
> Instead of holly, now up-raise
>   The greener box, for show.

> "The holly hitherto did sway ;
>   Let box now domineere ;
> Untill the dancing Easter-day,
>   Or Easter's eve appeare.

> "Then youthfull box which now hath grace,
>   Your houses to renew ;
> Grown old, surrender must his place,
>   Unto the crispèd yew.

> "When yew is out, then birch comes in,
>   And many flowers beside ;
> Both of a fresh and fragrant kinne
>   To honor Whitsuntide.

> " Green rushes then, and sweetest bents,
>   With cooler oken boughs,
>   Come in for comely ornaments
>   To re-adorn the house."

These manifold English pastimes, so largely a survival from heathen rites, were fostered by the Roman
Church until holy days passed into holidays, and soul
and sense kept festival together. England was
wonted to take her merry-makes as a gift from the
hand of Religion. A doggerel description of the festival of Corpus Christi, as observed in London, drawn
though it is by the grudging hand of an Elizabethan
Protestant, pictures the brightness and variety of that
none the less solemn procession.

> " There doth ensue the solemne feast of Corpus Christi Day,—
>   Who then can shewe their wicked use, and fonde and fool-
>   ish play?
>   The hallowed bread, with worship great, in silver Pix they
>   beare
>   About the Church, or in the Citie, passing here and theare.
>   His armes that beares the same, two of the welthiest men
>   do holde,
>   And over him a Canopey of silke and cloth of golde
>   Foure others use to beare aloufe, least that some filthie thing
>   Should fall from hie, or some mad bird her doung thereon
>   should fling.
>   Christes passion here derided is, with sundrie maskes and
>   playes.
>   Faire Ursley, with hir maydens all, doth passe amid the
>   wayes.

And, valiant George, with speare thou killed the dreadful
    dragon here,

The Devil's house is drawne about, wherein there doth
    appere

A wondrous sort of damned sprites, with foule and feareful
    looke,

Great Christopher doth wade and passe with Christ amid
    the brooke :

Sebastian full of feathred shaftes, the dint of dart doth feele.

There walketh Kathren, with hir sworde in hande, and
    cruel wheele :

The Challis and the singing Cake with Barbara is led,

And sundrie other pageants playde, in worship of this bred,

That please the foolish people well ; what should I stande
    upon

Their Banners, Crosses, Candlesticks and reliques many
    on,

Their Cuppes, and carved Images, that Priestes, with
    count'nance hie,

Or rude and common people, beare about full solemnlie ?

Saint John before the bread doth go, and poynting towardes
    him,

Doth shew the same to be the Lambe that takes away our
    sinne,

On whome two clad in Angels' shape do sundrie flowres
    fling,

A number great of sacring Belles with pleasant sound doe
    ring.

The common wayes with bowes are strawde, and every
    street beside,

And to the walles and windowes all, are boughes and
    brannches tide,

The monkes in every place do roame, the Nonnes abrode
    are sent,
The Priestes and schoolmen lowde do rore, some use the
    instrument.
The stranger passing through the streete, upon his knees
    doe fall :
And earnestly upon this bread, as on his God, doth call.
For why, they counte it for their Lorde, and that he doth
    not take
The forme of flesh, but nature now of breade that we do
    bake."

These church processions had a double dramatic
influence, promoting, on the one hand, the development of secular pageantry, which was so prominent a
feature of English life under the early kings, and, indeed, through the day of the Tudors, passing under
the Stuarts into the gorgeous masque ; and, on the
other hand, by their personations of sacred characters, yielding fresh impetus to the growth of the
religious drama.

The earliest play performed in England, of which
we have any record by name, is the *Ludus de S.
Katharina*, represented at Dunstable, very early in
the twelfth century, and perhaps written in French,
instead of Latin, its author being a Norman scholar,
one Geoffrey, a member of the University of Paris,
then resident in England. The question of its language must remain undecided, however, as the play
is lost. But there may well have been some popular

element in it to trouble the conscience of the play-wright, for his house taking fire and burning down the night after the representation, a clear sign of celestial displeasure, "he made himself," in the words of the old chronicler, a "holocaust," or propitiatory sacrifice, and took religious orders straightway, becoming, before he died, Abbot of St. Albans. According to the chronicle, a play like this was nothing new in England, but "de consuetudine magistrorum et scholarum." This testimony is confirmed by a few lines from Fitzstephen's *Life of Thomas à Becket*, written in the last quarter of the same century, the twelfth. Here, in a description of the metropolis, occurs the passage : "London, in lieu of the ancient shows of the theatre and the entertainments of the stage, has exhibitions of holier character, either representations of those miracles which holy confessors have wrought, or representations of those agonies through which the courage of the martyrs has shone bright."

The mention here is of Saint Plays, which would naturally follow close on the original Passion Plays ; for what could be more simple, after dramatic representation had once been introduced, than that, on the feast day of some Christian hero, whose martyrdom was stained in window, carved in canopy, and moulded in bas-relief, breathing figures should yet more vividly copy in action the story already before the eyes of the worshippers? Such living tableaux, pantomimes, and plays suitably illustrated the mediæval homily, which was not the tracing of an argument nor urging of a plea, but primarily the telling of a story. The mediæval preacher improved a saint-day by relating the usually apocryphal biography of the saint. But the plastic art must be held in the main responsible for tempting the drama to this extension of its sphere. It was as if the chiselled, painted saint himself, as a French savant has suggested, stepped down for an hour from marble niche or glowing window to play his life-drama once again in the cathedral nave, — for the Saint Plays did not venture within the sacred choir, but established themselves in the great body of the church, in the very midst of the crowding worshippers.

We find in England, in the earlier half of the twelfth century, three Latin plays, composed by Hilarius, an Englishman of French education, one of the many youths who flocked to the reed hut in the desert to learn scholastic philosophy of the famous Abelard. Of these dramas one, apparently a Christmas play, deals with the story of Daniel, another with the raising of Lazarus, and the third with a miracle of St. Nicholas, then, as now, a saint of wide and well-deserved popularity, the protector of the weak against the strong, and hence the peculiar patron of the young, especially of little children, dowerless maidens, and orphans. Mrs. Jameson avers that no other saint in the calendar has so many churches, chapels, and altars erected to him, the Greek church even exceeding the Latin in zeal to do him honour. Of all the legends that cluster about his name, that one most popular in the Middle Ages, although passed over by Hilarius in favour of another, forms the subject of one of the Saint Plays preserved in France, the manuscript bearing date of the twelfth century.

This play, which will serve as well as any for purposes of illustration, was probably introduced as an interlude into the matins or vespers of St. Nicholas' day. The plot is simplicity itself, involving but little action, and presenting three times over what is dramatically the same situation. A nobleman of a rueful countenance, accompanied by three maiden daughters, appears before the audience, and proceeds to bewail in sing-song Latin verses, the woes of poverty.

" My joy is turned to sorrow, my laughter to a sigh.
　What wealth was ours in happy years, those happy years
　　　gone by !
　　　　　Alack, alack the day !
　The pleasures of this mortal life have vanished quite away."

The maidens strive in vain to comfort their despondent parent, who obstinately refuses consolation : —

> " Once so rich, and now poorest of all,
>   Finding no solace by night nor by day,
>   Oh, I must suffer whatever befall,
>   Bearing my burden as well as I may."

The eldest daughter, moved by these incessant lamentations, desperately offers to devote herself to an infamous life, that her father and sisters may be saved from starvation.   But scarcely have the words left her lips, when a heavy purse of gold is thrown by an unseen hand at the feet of the father, whose spirits instantaneously rise to the occasion : —

> " Oh, my daughters, be happy with me !
>   The time of our trouble is over and spent,
>   For bountiful gold on the pavement I see,
>   Enough to suffice for our livelong content."

While the daughters are devoutly singing a psalm of thanksgiving, who should appear but a would-be son-in-law, a complacent young noble, who, eying the shining purse, introduces himself with not the faintest trace of embarrassment !

> " I am a man of record clear,
>   A man of well-approvèd life,
>   And I would make your daughter dear
>   My lawful wife."

The father, whose behaviour at this point is more modern than might be expected, refers the proposition to the lady.

> " Declare, my child, if you will wed
> This gallant youth, all gently bred,
> And handsome too."

The maiden, so spirited a moment before, responds with conventional meekness.

> " Be that, dear sir, as you shall say.
> I am your child to give away
> As pleases you."

The father benignantly places her hand in the hand of the wooer, and bestows the purse of gold as her dowry, — a most inconsiderate action, it would seem ; for no sooner have the twain departed, than he turns despairingly toward his two remaining children, and bewails his extremity of need in the very stanzas used before. The second daughter, although she has no hope to suggest, entreats her father not to sacrifice her to his necessity, but to endure all earthly suffering, rather than incur eternal punishment for sin. As she concludes her persuasions, again a purse of gold drops at the father's feet, again an opportune wooer presents himself, with the very words of his predecessor upon his lips, and the same dialogue as before takes place between the complaisant sire and the demure maiden.

The second purse of gold is given as dowry by this hopelessly improvident parent, who at once resumes his distressful chant more lustily than ever. But the third daughter has gained wisdom through these successive experiences, and she not only declines to sacrifice herself, but bids her father trust in God for deliverance.

> " For in Holy Writ are we clearly taught
>   That God will never forsake his own,
> But for those who love him are marvels wrought,
>   Wine of water and bread of stone."

At this point is heard the happy thump of the third purse of gold on the church pavement, and immediately after, to the enthusiastic joy of the audience, appears St. Nicholas himself, a bishop of amiable countenance, attired in gorgeous vestments. The enraptured father falls at his feet, the saint reveals his name, the daughter blesses God, the prospective son-in-law is not behindhand, the third betrothal takes place, the third dowry is bestowed, and the father, unmindful as ever of his own empty pockets, leads the choristers in a chant of praise to good St. Nicholas.

We can hardly call the Saint Plays a dramatic advance upon the Passion Plays, nor a distinct link in the chain of evolution. They are rather an off-shoot, a side-growth, gaining in freedom and originality, in that their less sacred material permitted some license on the part of the poet, but with the loss of the great theme losing heavily in dignity and beauty and essential dramatic quality. And yet, indirectly, they contributed to the development of religious drama through its original channel. For, as the Saint Plays grew to be more and more a feature of church festivals, new impetus was given to the Passion Plays, which gradually extended back, filling the gap between the Easter play and the Christmas play, through the life of our Lord, as if to include that, too, in the work of redemption; and further yet, back to the prophets and patriarchs who foretold and foreshadowed that life; back, still, to the fall of Adam, which made that atonement needful; back, still, to the fall of Lucifer, who wrought the fall of Adam. The Passion Play reached forward, too, from Easter morning to Ascension morning,—then to the Second Coming and the Judgment. There seems to have been at work, in all this, a dim sense of connecting first cause with final effect, of setting the Tree of Knowledge over against the Tree of Life.

The earliest manuscript yet discovered giving any sequence of Scripture plays dates from the twelfth century, and was preserved in France, at Tours. In this play there occurs, for the first time, mention of the stage as erected outside the church door,

God being represented, on descending from heaven, as coming out of the church. There is here some vivacity of dialogue, but the hymns of the choristers are still interblent with the scenes of the drama. None the less, this removal of the stage to the churchyard is of great significance. The liturgical Easter dramas were acted in the Holy of Holies, in the heart of the choir, under the very shadow of the High Altar. The Saint Plays slipped down into the nave, where they could be more generally witnessed; and then came the eventful step by which the theatre passed from under the vaulted roof, through the sculptured portal, out into the open air. No sooner were the plays established in the churchyards, than fairs, a new feature of medi-æval life, rose around them. All the out-lying neighbourhood would naturally be attracted to a reverend abbey, on the feast-day of its patron saint. It is good sometimes to hear Mass; sometimes to confess to the Holy Fathers and be shriven; some-times to lay an offering before the shrine; and what better occasion than the great spring festival? Moreover, if there be rheumatism in the shoulder, or sorrow in the heart, when would the saint be more likely to work his miracles?

With it all, there comes the longing for the con-course, for the merry fellowship, and for the play that is to be acted in the saint's honour, — the play that gives to toiling peasant-folk their one literary delight, their one intellectual stimulus of the circling year. So the people flocked from all about, clearing their consciences, indulging their social and æsthetic instincts, and soon learning, in those times of slow and insecure travel and hence of infrequent assemblage, to avail themselves of the opportunity for trade. But presently it came to pass that the hamlet about the abbey could not house all the guests of fair-time, so tents were pitched in the churchyard, and the tents soon grew into booths. By and by the churchyards were found too narrow to hold both the living and the dead, and stage and booths moved on together to large, open meadows, and then, at last, to the market-towns, where a movable stage was constructed that was wheeled from street to street. But now the Latin liturgical drama, — Passion Play and Saint Play alike, — is left far behind, and the English Miracle Cycle claims attention.

CHAPTER II.

MIRACLE PLAYS — DESCRIPTION.

THE Miracle Play was the training-school of the romantic drama. In England, during the slow lapse of some five centuries, the Miracle, with its tremendous theme and mighty religious passion, was preparing the day of the Elizabethan stage, for despite all crudities, prolixities, and absurdities of detail, these English Miracle Cycles are nobly dramatic both in range and spirit. In verbal expression they are almost invariably weak and bald, but on the mediæval scaffold-stage the actor counted for more than the author, and the religious faith and feeling of the audience filled in the homely lines with an unwritten poetry. Within the vast extent of these cyclic dramas, as within the length and breadth of the great cathedrals, there was room, however, for human life in all its various aspects. As the grotesque found place among the beautiful carvings of chapter-house and choir, so under the ample canopy of the old Miracle Play comedy grew up by the very side of tragedy, bringing the theatre at once into collision with the Church.

As long as the religious plays, although they had departed from the sacred edifice, remained under the exclusive control of the clergy, there was but little loss in solemn and tragic effect. Even in France, whose light and restless genius was the first to introduce a farcical element into the Mysteries, the Passion was acted with such intensity that, in one instance at least, the young priest personating Christ fainted on the cross. As for Germany, it is recorded that the play of the Foolish Virgins, presented at Eisenach, Easter, 1322, in the royal park, undermined with its horror the reason of the most distinguished beholder, the Landgrave Frederic of the Scarred Cheek. But it is not long before we find the Church regarding these out-of-door plays, whose language was fast slipping from Latin into the vernacular, with a doubtful countenance. By the middle of the thirteenth century, many of the bishops were inclined to prohibit the clergy from taking part in Mysteries set forth in "churchyards, streets, or green places," permitting them to act only in the liturgical dramas still played beneath the consecrated roofs at Christmas and at Easter. The way thus opened, a new class of actors came speedily to the front.

The conditions of feudal life, and the exactions of

the pleasure-loving Keltic temperament, had early brought into existence, on the Continent, a class of *joculatores*, men skilled in any or all of the several arts of minstrelsy, story-telling, dancing, jugglery, mimicry, and it was natural, — indeed, inevitable that the Miracle Plays, decorously and piously performed in the first instance by clergy within their ecclesiastical domains, should, as soon as they had ventured out from the "dim religious light" of choir and nave into the merry sunshine, be seized upon by these profane imitators, who soon became rivals and supplanters, too often turning what had been illustrated Scripture into scandal and buffoonery. The Norman conquest naturally scattered these Gallic *joculatores* or *histriones* over England, where they soon fell under ecclesiastical condemnation. But here the clergy, aided by the fact that these gay Frenchmen could not readily gain the ear of the humiliated, angry Saxon peasantry, held their own fairly well, and maintained the lead in the establishment of the national theatre. The priests, nevertheless, did not preserve their laurels as playwrights and actors without condescending to some of the tricks in trade of their opponents.

But by the time we find the English Miracle Cycles in full career, the clergy have ceased to be the customary actors. Yet the lower orders of the priesthood, however often forbidden by their ecclesiastical superiors, continued even down to the sixteenth century to bear some share in the representation of the Miracles, of which they remained, almost without exception, the authors and compilers. Regularly at London, and undoubtedly often elsewhere, the Miracles were performed by inferior personages attached to the Church, especially the parish clerks, like Chaucer's " Joly Absolon " of whom the poet says : —

> " Sometime to show his lightness and maistrie,
>   He plaieth Herod on a scaffold hie."

These parish clerks of London, of whom "Joly Absolon" is the immortal type, obtained in 1233 their charter as an harmonic guild and became a company of high repute, playing before Richard II., in 1390, and before Henry IV., in 1409, the performance on this latter occasion covering a period of eight days. But in many of the leading English towns, as York, Chester, Coventry, the trading guilds, by the close of the thirteenth century, had taken the task of setting forth the Miracles upon themselves. The conduct of these festivals was a matter of concern to the city corporations, too. At York, for instance, the council decreed in 1476: "That yerely in the tyme of lentyn there shall be called afore the maire for the tyme beying iiij of the moste connyng discrete and able players within this Citie, to serche, here, and examen all the plaiers and plaies and pagentes thrughoute all artificers belonging to Corpus Xt^i Plaie. And all suche as they shall fynde sufficiant in persone and connyng, to the honour of the Citie and worship of the saide Craftes, for to admitte and able; and all other insufficiant personnes, either in connyng, voice, or personne to discharge, ammove and avoide."

The best players being thus selected from among the followers of each craft, preparations began at once. Every guild became responsible for the presentation of a single pageant, or scene, furnishing its own movable stage, and meeting all the expenses of the pageant from its own treasury. The guilds acted as hosts to the entire neighbourhood, who rewarded by childlike interest and responsiveness the generosity of their entertainers. Each company appointed two pageant-masters, who controlled the pageant-silver, a fund made up by contributions from the members. The pageant-masters also superintended all the arrangements of the play, and trained the performers. One cannot think of these histrionic tradesmen without an amused remembrance of Shakespeare's irresistible burlesque, though Bully Bottom and his fellows represent a later stage of citizen actorship. When the arrangements for the play were perfected, a special "bayn," or crier, was sent around the city, usually twice, to announce it. The form of proclamation for the Corpus Christi plays, at York, ran as follows: —

" Proclamacio ludi corporis cristi facienda in virgilia corporis christi.

"Oiez, &c. We comand of ye kynges behalve and ye Mair and ye shirefs of yis Citee yat no mann go armed in yis Citee with swerdes ne with Carlill-axes, ne none other defences in distorbaunce of ye kynges pees and ye play, or hynderying of ye processioun of Corpore Christi, and yat yai leve yare hernas in yare Ines, saufand knyghtes and sqwyres of wirship yat awe have swerdes borne eftir yame, of payne of forfaiture of yaire wapen and imprisonment of yaire bodys. And yat men yat brynges furth pacentes yat yai play at the places yat is assigned yerfore and nowere elles, of ye payne of forfaiture to be raysed yat is ordayned yerfore, yat is to say xls. And yat menn of craftes and all othir menn yat fyndes torches, yat yai come furth in array and in ye manere as it has been used and customed before yis time, noght haveyng wapen, careynge tapers of ye pagentz. And officers yat ar keepers of the pees of payne of forfaiture of yaire fraunchis and yaire bodyes to prison : And all maner of craftmen yat bringeth furthe ther pageantez in order and course by good players, well arayed and openly spekyng, upon payn of lesyng of C.s to be paide to the chambre without any pardon. And that every player that shall play be redy in his pagiaunt at convenyant tyme, that is to say, at the mydhowre betwix iiij[th] and Vth of the cloke in the mornynge, and then all oyer pageantz fast followyng ilk one after oyer as yer course is, without tarieng. Sub pena facienda camere VI s. VIII d."

The division of scenes among the guilds is a curious and interesting matter. In the York pageants, for instance, one can hardly think it is all by accident that the plasterers were chosen for the representation of the creation of the earth, the shipwrights for the building of the ark, the fishmongers and mariners for the voyage of the ark, the "goldbeters" and "monemakers" for the adoration of the gift-bringing Magi, the vintners for the turning of the water into wine at Cana, and the bakers for the last supper. Nor are these all the examples that might be adduced, while, on the other hand, in many cases, there seems to be no such correspondence between the guild and the pageant.

This term *pageant* was originally applied, in England, to the movable platform which served as stage, the name soon passing over from the framework to the play exhibited upon it. The pageant scaffold was a wooden erection, set on wheels and divided into two stories, the lower serving as dressing-room, while the upper was the stage proper. The following words of Archdeacon Rogers, a sixteenth-century witness of the Whitsun Plays at Chester, describes clearly enough both the scaffold itself and the method of procedure : —

"The maner of these playes were, every company had his pagiant, wch pagiante weare a high scafold with 2 rowmes, a higher and a lower, upon 4 wheeles. In the lower they apparelled themselves, and in the higher rowme they played, beinge all open on the tope, that all behoulders might heare and see them. The places where they played them was in every streete. They began first at the Abay gates, and when the first pagiante was played, it was wheeled to the highe crosse before the Mayor, and so to every streete, and soe every streete had a pagiante playing before them at one time, till all the pagiantes for the daye appointed weare played, and when one pagiant was neere ended, worde was broughte from streete to streete, that soe they might come in place thereof, exceedinge orderly, and all the streetes have their pagiants afore them all at one time playeinge togeather ; to se w'ch playes was great resorte, and also scafolds and stages made in the streetes in those places where they determined to play theire pagiantes."

The French scaffold was more elaborate, presenting three platforms, one above another, with a black pit yawning beside the lowest. The highest platform was reserved for God the Father, God the Son, the Virgin Mary, and the angels. This was richly tapestried and furnished with trees and an organ. The second platform sufficed for saints, and the third represented earth, the pit beside it standing for "Hellmouthe," beheld as the gaping jaws, sometimes worked so as to open and shut, of a hideous monster, fondly supposed to resemble a whale. In Germany, comparatively little care was bestowed upon accessories. There heaven was located at one end of the platform, raised by a few steps above the level which represented earth, while, in some cases, at least, a huge cask had to do duty as hell, the Devil leaping in and out of this with as much agility as he could command. Another cask, set upside down, served as the Mount of Temptation or Transfiguration.

The difference between France and England in the arrangement of the pageant-house, the English scaffold presenting but one open stage, with the story below curtained off as a green-room, and the French scaffold exposing three stages, the respective abodes of Deity and angels, of saints, and of men, was instrumental in differentiating the rôle of devils in the two countries. These personages, to be sure, had their proper abode in hellmouth; but whereas, in England, the dragon-jaws emitted the devils only when they had some dismal task to perform, in France, while the scene of action was, for the time being, on one of the upper stages, the devils were accustomed to pop out of their prison, run across the human stage, and even leap down among the audience, playing tricks and executing gambols. So the French devils degenerated into drolls, while the English and German, though equally grotesque in appearance, aimed at producing impressions of terror, rather than of mirth. Into hellmouth, from which smoke and flame continually arose, these English demons, bristling with horsehair, and wearing beast heads, the ugliest possible,—always a prominent item in the bill of costs,—dragged with much mockery and show of cruelty those souls whose black, red, and yellow coats, suggestive of the fire that awaited them, indicated their fitness for such habitation. Souls destined for heaven wore white coats and white hose, and the angels, duly plumed, were resplendent in gold. The high priests, Annas and Caiaphas, wore ecclesiastical robes, often borrowed from the church. The Virgin and the other Marys wore crowns. Herod was gay in blue satin gown, and gilt and silvered helmet, with various Saracenic accoutrements, as the crooked falchion. Pilate wore a green robe, and carried a leather club stuffed with wool. The tormentors of Christ wore jackets of black buckram, painted over with nails and dice. Our Lord was represented in a coat of white sheepskin, variously painted, with red sandals, the sandals of one who had trodden the winepress, and gilt peruke and beard. Gilt perukes and beards were worn by all the apostles, also, and by other saints whom the people were accustomed to see emblazoned on church walls, or windows, with a halo about the head. Judas was distinguished by his red beard and yellow robe. The most striking costume was that of the devil, who was as shaggy and beast-like as possible, black, horned, clawed, with cloven feet and a forked tail, and, sometimes, with pipes of burning gunpowder in his ears.

The bills of expense, which have been discovered at Coventry and elsewhere, throw much light on the stage accessories and wardrobes. In the lists of gar-

ments provided for the principal characters, we come
upon some names among the *dramatis personæ* that
the gospel reader would hardly expect, such as Pilate's
Son, Herod's Son, Bishops, Beadle, Mother of Death,
and Worms of Conscience. Records like the following, too, though penned in all devout simplicity, fall
strangely on the modern ear.

Paid for a pair of gloves for God . . . . . . 2d.
Paid for four pair of angels' wings . . . . . . 2s. 8d.
Paid for nine and a half yards of buckram for the
    souls' coats . . . . 7s.
Paid for ale when the players dress them . . . . 4d.
Paid for painting and making new hell head . . . 12d.
Paid for mending of hell head . . . . 6d.
Paid for keeping hell head . . . . 8d.
Paid for a pair of new hose and mending of the old
    for the white souls . . . . 18d.
Paid for mending the garment of Jesus, and the
    cross painting . . . . 1s. 3d.
Paid for a pound of hemp to mend the angels' heads 4d.
Paid for linen cloth for the angels' heads and Jesus'
    hose, making in all . . . . 9d.
Paid for washing the lawn bands for the Saints in
    the church . . . . 2d.
To Fawston for hanging Judas . . . . 4d.
To Fawston for cockcrowing . . . . 10d.
   Item : Painting of the world.
   Item : Link for setting the world on fire.
   Item : Girdle for God.
   Item : For mending the demon's head.

Item : Chevrel (apparently peruke) for God.

Item : Two chevrels gilt for Jesus and Peter.

Item : A cloak for Pilate.

Item : Pollaxe for Pilate's son.

Item : To reward Mistress Grimsby for lending of her gear to Pilate's wife.

Item : Divers necessaries for the trimming of the Father of Heaven.

Among the stage effects we find : —

A gilded cross with a rope to draw it up and a curtain to hang before it.

Scourges and a gilded pillar.

Trumpets and bagpipes.

A cord for Judas to hang himself.

Rock. Tomb. Spade. Rushes. Censers. Stars. Diadems.

Standard made of red buckram.

Starch to make a storm.

The barrel for the earthquake.

Pulpits for the angels.

But, however grotesque all this may seem to-day, there is good reason for believing that the English throngs drawn by these Pageants to the market-towns on high church festivals looked and listened to their æsthetic and spiritual edification. In France, where the performance of a series of Mysteries was undertaken by the town, irrespective of the guilds, all the people were eager to bear part in the representation, regarding such acting as a religious service, to be counted unto the actor for righteousness. A solemn trumpet-call, *le cri du jeu*, would summon all who might desire, for the glory of Christ, or the weal of their own souls, to assist in the representation. The volunteers placed in the hands of the magistrate a signed paper, wherein they made oath, on pain of death, or forfeiture of property, to study carefully the rôle assigned, and to be promptly on hand on the day of representation. Those of the ignorant rabble, who, eager to show some grace to Christ, and win His grace in return, flocked after the trumpet, were massed as Israelites in the wilderness, or the mob about the cross. Sometimes, half the town acted, while the other half looked on, together with the rustics of the outlying villages. But, even so, there was no entrance fee, although gifts to aid in defraying expenses were acceptable, not only on earth, but in heaven, such gifts partaking of the nature of a religious offering.

Yet, notwithstanding this truly devotional spirit, the rude, laughter-loving tastes of the populace so wrought upon the playwrights as to bring about the introduction of certain distinctly comic episodes into the sacred history. In the English cycles, the fun is chiefly furnished, in the Old Testament plays, by the buffoonery between Cain and his ploughboy, and by the shrill insubordination of Noah's wife, when the patriarch would persuade her to enter the ark; while

to the story of the Saviour's life and death, evidently
regarded then, as by the peasants of Oberammergau
to-day, in the light of solemn and heart-moving tragedy, a foil was afforded by the clownish talk and
actions of the shepherds. That this food for mirth
was sometimes of the coarsest should not be taken as
proving intentional irreverence on the part of players
or of hearers. It points to social rather than moral
causes. The conditions of family life for the lower
classes of the English, in the years when Chaucer
and Langland wrote, and Miracle Plays were in full
tide of popularity, precluded delicacy of manners or
of speech.

As a representative Miracle Cycle I would select
the Towneley Mysteries, sometimes styled the Widkirk or Woodkirk Plays. The first of these two
names, for Widkirk and Woodkirk are essentially the
same word, is taken from Towneley Hall in Lancashire, where the manuscript was preserved. The
second is derived from a vague tradition that this
old parchment volume before coming, at an unknown
date and under long-forgotten circumstances, into
possession of the Towneley family, belonged to the
"Abbey of Widkirk, near Wakefield, in the county
of York." No modern research has succeeded in tracing any such abbey, or any place of that name in
York, or, indeed, anywhere in England ; but it appears
that about four miles from the old town once known

as "Merry Wakefield," where plays would naturally have been acted, there did exist a place called Woodkirk, which harboured, before the dissolution of the monasteries, a small religious brotherhood, a cell of Augustinian or Black Canons, subject to the flourishing house of St. Oswald, at Nostel. The dialect of all these Mysteries save four ("Processus Prophetarum," "Pharao," "Cæsar Augustus," "Annunciatio") reveals a Yorkshire origin, one or two local allusions occur, and the words "Wakefelde Barkers" (tanners), "Glover Pageant," "Fysher Pageant," written over three of the plays, would seem to warrant the conclusion that these Mysteries were composed, or adapted from a lost original, by the Woodkirk monks and acted by the trade-guilds of Wakefield at the fairs which, as old charters show, were sometimes held on occasion of high church festivals, in that town. Each guild had a particular pageant assigned it for representation, and, probably, no less than three days were required to complete the series, which numbers thirty plays in order, from the "Creation" to the "Judgment Day," with two later additions, "Lazarus" and the "Hanging of Judas." These Mysteries, whose conjectural date is the fourteenth century, or even earlier, are rude but often forceful and vivacious in composition, familiar in style, dialectical in diction, and enlivened at intervals by the broadest kind of humour.

We must imagine an open market-place, in the centre of a mediæval English town, — rows of quaint, narrow, gabled houses, whose windows are alive with faces, closing in the square, which is thronged by a motley multitude, — Yorkshire rustics, green-clad yeomen, young clerks and squires in many-coloured, picturesque costumes, gowned and hooded friars, ker-chiefed women, here and there a knight in glistening mail, everywhere beggars, children, dogs, all pressing toward the lofty stage adorned with crosses and streamers, which rises in the centre of the scene. On the upper platform, from whose edges rich drap-eries, wrought with Christian emblems, fall to conceal the dressing-room below, appears the white-vested, golden-haired figure of the Creator, seated upon a throne, and surrounded by His cherubim. He speaks : —

> " Ego sum Alpha et O,
> I am the first and last also,
> Oone God in mageste ;
> Marvelose, of myght most,
> Fader, and Sone, and Holy Ghost,
> One God in Trinyte."

In this same abrupt, prentice-like measure the Deity continues with assurances of His eternity, omniscience and omnipotence, His firm determina-tion to maintain all these, and, finally, with an exceedingly succinct account of the creation, as

He performs it on the stage by aid of lanterns, hawthorn branches, and wooden images of birds and beasts. The conception of the creative process is no less crude and childish than these illustrations themselves; the narrative is of the baldest, and the grammatical construction absolutely ragged. But as the cherubim break forth in a choral address to God, we are aware of a lighter movement, a freer fancy, and a distinct dramatic intent in the introduction, somewhat precipitate though it seems, of the praises of Lucifer.

> " Oure Lord God in trynyte,
> Myrth and lovyng be to the,[1]
> Myrth and lovyng over al thyng ;
> For thou has made, with thi bidyng,
> Heven, and erth, and alle that is,
> And giffen us joy that never shalle mys.
> Lord, thou art fulle mych[2] of myght,
> That has maide Lucifer so bright.
> We love the,[1] Lord, bright are we,
> But none of us so bright as he.
> He may well hight[3] Lucifer,
> For luffy light that he doth bere."

This anthem has an intoxicating effect upon the archangel's pride, and no sooner has God arisen from His throne and begun to walk toward the rear of the stage, than Lucifer usurps the vacant

---

[1] thee. [2] much. [3] be called.

seat, appealing to his fellows to know if it does not become him as well as the Creator.

> " Say, fellows, how semys now me
>   To sit in seyte of trynyte?
> I am so bright of ich a lym,[1]
> I trow me seme as welle as hym."

But the angels divide upon this question, and Lucifer, proposing to display his powers still further, attempts to fly off the stage and disastrously falls into hellmouth, his adherents tumbling after. These bad angels, who are henceforth designated as demons, and who, perhaps, have torn off their outer robes of white on alighting in the pit and revealed inner garments black and ragged, raise cries of dismay and reproach.

> "Alas, alas, and wele-wo !
>   Lucifer, why felle thou so?
> We, that were angels so fare,
> And sat so hie above the ayere,
> Now ar we waxen blak as any coylle."

The scene is presently transferred to the upper stage. God re-enters, or advances from the background, and without offering the slightest comment on past events, resumes His throne and tranquilly proceeds with His interrupted task of creation. Adam is moulded out of clay, and into him is breathed the divine life. A rib is taken from his

---

[1] every lineament.

side and transformed into a helpmate for him.   The
keeping of the garden is entrusted to the pair,
with strict injunction as to the forbidden tree.

Deus.   Erthly bestes, that may crepe and go,
      Bryng ye furth and wax ye mo,
        I see that it is good ;
      Now make we man to our liknes,
      That shalle be keper of more and les,
        Of fowles, and fysh in flood.
              (*Et tanget eum.*)
      Spreyte of life I in the blaw,
      Good and ille both shalle thou knaw ;
        Rise up, and stand bi me.
      Alle that is in water or land,
      It shalle bow unto thi hand,
        And sufferan shalle thou be ;
      I gif the witt, I gif the strength,
      Of alle thou sees, of brede and lengthe ;
        Thou shalle be wonder wise.
      Myrth and joy to have at wille,
      Alle thi likyng to fulfille,
        And dwelle in paradise.
      This I make thi wonnyng playce,[1]
      Fulle of myrth and of solace,
        And I seasse [2] the therin.
      It is not good to be alone,
      To walk here in this worthely wone,[3]
        In alle this welthly wyn [4] ;
      Therfor, a rib I from the take,

---

[1] dwelling-place.   [2] establish.   [3] dwelling.   [4] joy in possession.

Therof shalle be thi make,
　　And be to thi helpyng.
Ye both to governe that here is,
And ever more to be in blis,
　　Ye wax in my blissyng.
Ye shalle have joye and blis therin,
While ye wille kepe you out of syn,
　　I say without lese.[1]
Ryse up, myn angelle cherubyn,
Take and leyd theym both in,
　　And leyf them there in peasse.

(*Tunc capit Cherubyn Adam per manum, et dicet eis Dominus.*)

Here thou Adam, and Eve thi wife,
I forbede you the tre of life,
And I commaund, that it begat,
Take which ye wille, bot negh[2] not that.
Adam, if thou breke my rede,
Thou shalle dye a dulfulle[3] dede.

Cherubyn. Oure Lord, our God, thi wille be done ;
I shalle go with theym fulle sone.
For soth, my Lord, I shalle not sted
Tille I have theym theder led.
We thank the Lord, with fulle good chere,
That has maide man to be oure peere,[4]
Com furth, Adam, I shalle the leyd,
Take tent to me, I shalle the reyd.
I rede the thynk how thou art wroght,
And luf my Lord in alle thi thoght,
That has maide the thrugh his wille,
Angels ordir to fulfille,

---

[1] lies.　　　[2] approach.　　　[3] doleful.　　　[4] companion.

> Many thynges he has the giffen,
> And made the master of alle that lyffen,
> He has forbed the bot a tre ;
> Look that thou let it be,
> For if thou breke his commaundment,
> Thou skapys not bot thou be shent.[1]
> Weynd[2] here in to paradise,
> And luke now that ye be wyse,
> And kepe you welle, for I must go
> Unto my Lord, there I cam fro.

Adam. Almyghte Lord, I thank it the
> That is, and was, and shalle be,
> Of thy luf and of thi grace,
> For now is here a mery place ;
> Eve, my felow, how thynk the this?

Eve. A stede me thynk of joye and blis,
> That God has giffen to the and me,
> Withoutten ende ; blissyd be he.

Adam. Eve, felow, abide me thore,
> For I wille go to viset more,
> To se what trees that here been ;
> Here are welle moo then we have seen,
> Greses, and othere smalle floures,
> That smelle fulle swete, of seyre[3] colours.

Adam, thus overcome by his masculine curiosity, leaves Eve unprotected, while he starts off on a tour of exploration about his new domain. Even as he departs, the menacing voice of the ruined archangel rises from the fiery cavern, and although four leaves

---

[1] punished.   [2] wend.   [3] several.

of the manuscript are here torn away, we can easily imagine the temptation and the fall as enacted by the Wakefield tanners in the listening market-place.

The Eden scaffold is now drawn onward to the head of the first street, where, although still so early in the morning, an impatient concourse has been waiting for an hour past. Before the recent spectators have turned their eyes from the disappearing platform, a second pageant-carriage, upon which is to be enacted one of the liveliest miracles of the series, rolls into the square. The audience greets this platform, furnished and decorated by the glovers of Wakefield, with vociferous applause, which is promptly rebuked by the first character who steps out upon the stage, a mirth-provoking personage, unknown to the writer of Genesis, but familiar to mediæval playgoers under the title of Garcio, or Cain's ploughboy. His saucy speech forms a rough prologue to the pageant, which actually opens with the appearance of Cain. The first murderer presents himself, not upon the scaffold, but in a reserved space of ground at its foot, where he is ploughing with a contrary team of mingled horses and oxen, and cursing the boy for the waywardness of the beasts. The boy, glorying in his mischief, acknowledges that he has filled the cattle's feeding-racks with stones, whereupon the ill-tempered Yorkshire rustic deals him a fisticuff in the face, straightway receiving as good as he sent. They are

in the midst of a tussle, when Abel enters, with
gentle words of greeting.

> " God as he bothe may and can
>   Spede the, brothere, and thi man."

Cain's response is of the rudest insolence, but
Abel, deprecating his wrath, urges the surly ploughman to go with him to sacrifice. Cain doggedly
maintains that he owes God nothing.

> "When alle mens corne was fayre in feld
>   Then was myne not worthe an eld ;
>   When I should saw,[1] and wantyd seyde,
>   And of corne had fulle grete neyde,
>   Then gaf he me none of his,
>   No more wille I gif hym of this."

But Abel's entreaty finally prevails, and Cain,
grumbling at every step, reluctantly follows his
brother out of the half-ploughed field, and up a hill,
which the scaffold represents. Here Abel offers his
sacrifice with reverent prayer, upon which breaks in
the harsh voice of Cain, his own address to God being
as blunt and gruff as his speech to his fellow-men.
The audience derives great delight from these defiant
orisons, and from the grudging fashion in which Cain
slowly selects the worst of his sheaves for the altar.

> " But now begyn wille I then,
>   Syn I must nede my tend to bren.[2]

[1] sow.   [2] tithe to burn.

Oone shefe, oone, and this makes two,
Bot nawder of thise may I forgo ;
Two, two, now this is thre,
Yei, this also shalle leif withe me ;
For I wille chose and best have,
This hold I thrift of alle this thrafe[1] ;
Wemo, wemo, foure, lo, here !
Better groved[2] me no this yere.
At yere tyme I sew fare corn,
Yit was it siche when it was shorne,
Thystyls and breyrs yei grete plente,
And alle kyn wedes that myght be.
Foure shefes, foure ; lo, this makes fyfe,
Deylle I fast thus long or I thrife,
Fyfe and sex, now this is seven, —
But this gettes never God of heven,
Nor none of thise foure, at my myghte,
Shalle never com in Godes sight.
Seven, seven, now this is aght."

But here Abel, piously shocked, interposes.

Abelle. Cain, brother, thou art not God betaght.[3]
Cayn. We therfor, is it that I say?
For I wille not deyle my good away ;
Bot had I gyffen him this to teynd
Then wold thou say he were my freynd,
But I thynk not, bi my hode,
To departe so lightly fro my goode.
We, acht, acht, and neyn, and ten is this,
We, that may we best mys.

---

[1] twenty-four sheaves.   [2] grew.   [3] submissive.

Gif Him that that lighes thore ;
It goyse agans myn hart fulle sore.

*   *   *   *   *   *

Abelle. Caine, of God me thynke thou has no drede.
Cayn. Now and He get more, the deville me spede,
As mych as oone reepe,
For that cam hym fulle light cheap ;

*   *   *   *   *   *

For that, and this that lyys here,
Have cost me fulle dere ;
Or it was shorne, and broght in stak,
Had I many a wery bak ;
Therfor aske me no more of this,
For I have giffen that my wille is.

Abelle. Cain, I rede thou tend right
For drede of hym that sittes on hight.

And now Cain's fatal wrath begins to burn against
his brother.

Cayn. How that I tend, rek the never a deille,
Bot tend thi skabbid shepe wele ;
For if thou to my teynd tent take
It bese the wars for thi sake.
Thou wold I gaf hym this shefe, or this sheyfe,
Na nawder of thise two will I leife ;
Bot take this now, has he two,
And for my saulle now mot it go,
Bot it gos sore agans my wille,
And shal he like fulle ille.

Abelle. Cain, I reyde thou so teynd
That God of heven be thi freynd.

Cayn. My freynd? na, not bot if he wille!
        I did hym neveryit bot skille.[1]
        If he be never so my fo
        I am avised gif hym no mo;
        Bot channge thi conscience, as I do myn,
        Yit teynd thou not thy mesel[2] swyne?
Abelle. If thou teynd right thou mon it fynde.

At this suggestion, with all that it implies, the
rage of Cain blazes hotter than before.

Cayn. The deville hang the bi the nek;
        How that I teynd never thou rek.
        Wille thou not yit hold thi peasse?
        Of this janglyng I reyde thou seasse.
        And teynd I welle, or tend I ille,
        Bere the even and speke bot skille.
        Bot now syn thou has teyndid thyne,
        Now wille I set fyr on myne.
        We, out, haro, help to blaw!
        It wille not bren for me, I traw;
        Puf, this smoke dos me myche shame,
        Now bren, in the devillys name.
        A, what deville of helle is it?
        Almost had myne brethe beyn dit.[3]
        Had I blawen oone blast more
        I had beyn choked right thore.

And while Cain, coughing and cursing, staggers
back from the altar, Abel, who, in disregard of his

[1] reason.   [2] measly.   [3] stopped.

brother's angry warnings, has lingered near the scene, cries with sorrowful foreboding : —

> *Abelle.* Cain, this is not worthe oone leke ;
> Thy tend should bren with outten smeke.

The answer vouchsafed to his fraternal solicitude is a furious snarl from the still choking and gasping husbandman.

> *Cayn.* For the it brens but the wars.
> I wold that it were in thi throte,
> Fyre, and shefe, and iche a sprote.[1]

Then upon the ears of the reckless blasphemer falls a still, small voice, — never before or since, we may well believe, more irreverently greeted.

> *Deus.* Cain, why art thou so rebelle
> Agans thi brother Abelle ?
> *Caym.* Whi, who is that Hob over the walle ?
> We, who was that that piped so smalle ?
> Com, go we hens, for perels alle ;
>   God is out of hys wit.
> Com furth, Abelle, and let us weynd,
> Me thynk that God is not my freynd,
>   On land then wille I flyt.[2]
> *Abelle.* O, Caym, brother, that is ille done.
> *Caym.* No, bot go we hens sone ;
> And if I may, I shalle be
>   Ther as God shalle not me see.

---

[1] every sprout.   [2] flee.

Poor Abel, not daring to openly oppose the wild will of the outcast, in a feeble and *mal apropos* fashion proposes to go and feed the cattle.

> *Abelle.*   Dere brother, I wille fayre
>   On feld ther oure bestes ar,
>   To looke if thay be holgh[1] or fulle.

Over Cain's tumult of passions his wrath, waxed dark and murderous, now obtains the mastery.

> *Cayn.*   Na, na abide, we have a craw to pulle ;
>   Hark, speke with me or thou go,
>   What wenys thou to skape so?
>   We, na, I aght the a fowlle dispyte,
>   And now is tyme that I hit qwite.
> *Abel.*   Brother, whi art thou so to me in ire?
> *Caym.*   We, theyf, whi brend thi tend so shyre[2]?
>   Ther myne did bot smoked
>   Right as it wold us bothe have choked.
> *Abel.*   Godes wille I trow it were
>   That myn brened so clere ;
>   If thyne smoked am I to wite[3]?

With this Cain leaps upon his brother, apparently anticipating, as implement for the slaughter, the famous weapon of Samson.

> *Caym.*   We, yei, that shal thou sore abite ;
>   Withe cheke bon, or that I blyn,[4]
>   Shal I the and thi life twyn.[5]

---

[1] hollow.   [2] sheer.   [3] blame.   [4] cease.   [5] separate.

> So lig down ther and take thi rest,
> Thus shalle shrewes be chastysed best.
>
> *Abel.* Venjance, venjance, Lord, I cry ;
> For I am slayne, and not gilty.

The fratricide accomplished, Cain taunts his silent victim yet again, turns glowering upon the audience, and then, suddenly overcome by the terrors of conscience, creeps quakingly into a convenient hole provided on the stage. But the voice of God pursues him there.

> *Deus.* Caym ! Caym !
> *Caym.* Who is that that callis me ?
> I am yonder, may thou not se ?
> *Deus.* Caym, where is thi brother Abelle ?
> *Caym.* What askes thou me ?   I trow at helle ;
> At helle I trow he be,
> Who so were ther then myght he se,
> Or som where fallen on slepyng ;
> When was he in my kepyng ?
> *Deus.* Caym, Caym, thou was wode[1] ;
> The voyce of thi brotheres blode
> That thou has slayn, on fals wise,
> From erthe to heven vengeance cryse.
> And, for thou has broght thi brother down,
> Here I gif the my malison.

With this the play reaches its true dramatic conclusion, and up to this point, for all the naiveté, the rudeness and grossness of language and action,

---

[1] mad.

there has been spirit, vigour, and even a just dramatic progression. The continual mounting of Cain's passionate temper, under Abel's well-intended but somewhat priggish admonitions, is well depicted, and the boy, with his ready sauce, his monkey play, and frank flavour of democracy, furnishes a needed foil to the tragic elements in the drama. The peculiar value of Cain, as a character, lies in his reality. We feel that this Cain is true, not indeed to oriental legend, but to human nature, as exhibited among Yorkshire boors in Chaucer's century. This fierce and niggardly ploughman, who might as well be called Dick or Robin, would be at home in the procession of Canterbury pilgrims, where he would find bullies, blusterers, and rascals, quite of his own crow-feather, and among these another ploughman of that Christ-type, which redeems even the type of Cain.

But the play fails utterly here at the dramatic climax. It is unable to rise to the tragic opportunity. It falls back foolishly, instead, on an iteration of Cain's sulky temper and the boy's buffoonery, until the scene degenerates into open farce. Then the pageant-carriage is wheeled away, not without having impressed its moral lesson. More than one foul-mouthed, violent-handed rustic in that holiday throng will remember for a few weeks or so to pay his farthings to the priest with fewer curses and use his heavy fist more sparingly.

These two opening pageants are fairly representative both of Miracles in general and of the Towneley collection in particular. The first illustrates the more conventional treatment of Biblical story — or what was supposed to be Biblical story, — the second the freer and more humorous. Of the remaining pageants we can let ourselves catch but glimpses, as the thirty glittering scaffolds roll in and out of Wakefield market-square.

There is the popular Noah pageant, with its white-haired patriarch lamenting over the sins of the world, God descending from heaven and bidding him build the ark of refuge, the taunts of Noah's shrewish wife, the lively scuffle that ensues between these venerable worthies, heads of the only virtuous household left on earth, and the laborious building of the ark by the rheumatic old shipwright. But even then his stubborn dame refuses to leave her spinning on the hilltop, until the waves swash over her feet, and she comes bounding into the ark in terror of her life. Here, one regrets to record, Noah welcomes her with a severe flogging, because of her previous contumacy. She retaliates by calling him names, Wat Wynd and Nicholle Nedy, stoutly refusing to sue for mercy, although she is " bet so blo " that she wishes her husband dead and the husbands, likewise, of all

the women in the audience.   Noah, too, turns to the
assembly with the sententious counsel : —

> " Ye men that has wifes, whyles they are yong,
>   If ye luff your lives, chastice thare tong."

The following pageant sets forth the story of Abraham and Isaac, and, although the treatment is discur-
sive and the text nowhere markedly poetical, the
simple drama is not without a homely English beauty
of its own.   The childish docility of the boy, and the
unavailing efforts of the submissive, bewildered father
to strike the fatal blow are clearly realised.

Isaac.   What have I done, fader, what have I saide?
Abraham.   Truly, no kyns ille to me.
Isaac.   And thus gyltles shalle be arayde?
Abraham.   Now, good son, let siche wordes be.
Isaac.   I luf you ay.
Abraham.   So do I thee.
Isaac.   Fader !
Abraham.   What, son?
Isaac.   Let now be seyn
For my moder luf.
Abraham.   Let be, let be !
It wille not help that thou wold meyn ;
Bot ly stylle tille I com to the,
I mys a lytylle thyng, I weyn.
He spekes so rufully to me
That water shotes in both myn eeyn,
I were lever than alle warldly wyn,
That I had fon him onys unkynde,

But no defawt I faund hym in ;
I wold be dede for hym or pynde.
To slo hym thus I thynk grete syn,
So rufulle wordes I with hym fynd ;
I am fulle wo that we shuld twyn,[1]
For he wille never oute of my mynd.
What shal I to hys moder say?

The fifth pageant shows Jacob stealing the blessing and fleeing from the wrath of Esau. The sixth
pageant sets forth in manner decorous and dull,
without much action or effort at characterisation,
Jacob's dream, his wrestling with the Angel and his
reconciliation with Esau. The seventh pageant is
rather a pomp than a play. Moses, rehearsing the
ten commandments, David, quoting from the psalms,
the Roman Sibyl, — a prophetic figure not unfamiliar
to the Mysteries, — and the prophet Daniel all fore-
tell, one after another, the coming of the Christ.

" Of a madyn shalle he be borne,
    To save alle that ar forlorne,
    Ever more withoutten end."

The Old Testament pageants close with the story
of Moses, who first appears in shepherd garb, inform-
ing the audience that he is now

    " set to kepe
Under thys montayn syde,
Byschope Jettyr shepe,"

[1] part.

but presently confounds Pharaoh and his magicians, calls down the ten plagues, and leads the Israelites in safety through the Red Sea.

The first of the New Testament platforms is occupied by Cæsar Augustus, a vainglorious bully, who ingratiates himself with the audience by offering to behead any one of them who dares utter a word during the pageant. His rage and dismay, on learning from his two councillors that a child is to be born in Judea who shall excel him in glory, are absurdly extravagant. He sends his messenger "Lyghtfote" to bid his cousin, Sir Siranus, attend him, and to this sage knight confides his anxiety. Sir Siranus suggests that a general poll-tax, or "heede penny," be decreed, and Cæsar prays the messenger, as he "luffes Mahowne," to speed that mandate on. The Annunciation Pageant follows, God avowing that He will visit the long affliction of Adam His handiwork with "oylle of mercy."

> "For he has boght his syn fulle sore,
> Thise V thousand yeris and more,
> Fyrst in erth, and sythen in helle."

Gabriel is despatched to bear to Mary the mystic salutation.

> "Angelle must to Mary go,
> For the feynd was Eve fo ;
> He was foule and layth to syght,
> And thou art angelle fayr and bright."

The pageant dwells less upon the visit of Gabriel to Mary, however, than upon the perturbations of simple old Joseph, who lends to these earlier Gospel scenes a touch of mingled pathos and comedy. The *Salutation* consists of a brief dialogue between Mary and Elizabeth, pleasing for the unwonted ease of the verse and for the loving courtesy of woman to woman.

Maria. My lord of heven, that syttys he,
And alle thyng seys withe eee,
The safe, Elezabethe.

Elezabethe. Welcom, Mary, blyssed blome,
Joyfulle am I of thi com,
To me, from Nazarethe.

Maria. How standes it with you, dame, of quart?[1]

Elezabethe. Welle, my doghter and dere hart,
As can for myn elde.

* * * * *

Fulle lang shalle I the better be,
That I may speke my fylle with the,
My dere kyns woman;
To wytt how thi freyndes fare,
In thi countre where thay ar,
Therof telle me thou can,
And how thou farys, my dere derlyng.

Maria. Welle, dame, gramercy youre askyng,
For good I wote ye spyr.[2]

Elezabethe. And Joachym, thy fader, at hame,
And Anna, my nese, and thi dame,
How standes it with hym and hir?

---

[1] spirits.   [2] question.

> *Maria.*   Dame, yit ar thay bothe on lyfe,
>   Bothe Joachym and Anna his wyfe.
> *Elezabethe.*   Else were my hart fulle sare.

The next two pageants, both dealing with the
nightwatch and adoration of the shepherds, serve as
a farcical interlude between the tender gravity of the
plays immediately preceding, and the solemnity, deepening into tragedy, of the plays to come. These two
comedies are not in sequence, but independent versions of the shepherd story. The leading characters
of the former are a group of Yorkshire boors, Gyb,
John Horne, and Slow-Pace, preposterous simpletons
all three, and Jak Garcio, a rough fellow of a shrewder
cast. After much grumbling and quarrelling, and
after a supper of such coarse scraps as each has
begged during the day, they say their extraordinary
prayers and go to sleep. Startled awake by the
angel's song, they fall to naïve discussion of the
Gloria, and ludicrous attempts to imitate it. At last,
they are guided by the star in the east to the manger
of Bethlehem, where, like the very clowns they are,
they linger bashfully about the door, each pushing
his fellow forward. But, once in presence of the
Child, they fall on their knees, and eagerly tender
their simple gifts, — a little spruce coffer, a ball, and
a bottle. The other *Pagina Pastorum* is an equally
remarkable instance of historical incongruity, being
another rude, realistic sketch of Northumbrian shep-

herd life in the days of the early Edwards. This rol-
licking farce was undoubtedly the favourite pageant
of the series, greeted with clamorous applause as it
moved from street to street. Here, too, the introductory characters are three shepherds, the weather-
beaten Colle, the hen-pecked Gyb, and the boy
Daw, who is something of a rogue. But the prime
rogue of the comedy is Mak, a lazy, lawless vagabond, ready to shift sail with every wind that blows,
and well mated in his wife Gylle, a scold and a
slut, who sharpens her tongue on her husband early
and late, letting the larder shelves, which his thrift-
lessness keeps bare, be overrun by spiders. But
it is impossible not to delight in this scampish,
hungry, fun-loving Mak, whose character is cleverly
and consistently sketched from his first appearance
on the moor, by mischance, before the shepherds
whom he has it in heart to rob, and whose recognition he tries to escape by muffling himself in his
cloak and disguising his voice, to the final detec-
tion in his cottage, where, the stolen sheep being
tucked away as a new-born baby in the cradle,
he brazens out the situation with one lie clapped
upon another, and, when nothing else will suffice,
with a promise of amendment,—the greatest lie of
all.

The shepherds, who, on discovering the loss of the
sheep, instantly turn their suspicions upon Mak and

his wife, are about to leave the cottage after a fruit-
less quest : —

Tercius Pastor.   Alle wyrk we in vayn ! as welle may we go.
     But hatters,[1]
   I can fynde no flesh
   Hard nor nesh,[2]
   Salt nor fresh,
     Bot two tome[3] platters.

*   *   *   *   *

Uxor.   No, so God me blys, and gyf me joy of
     my chylde.
Primus Pastor.   We have marked amys ; I hold us begyld.
Secundus Pastor.   Syr, don.
   Syr, oure lady hym save.
   Is youre chyld a knave ?[4]
Mak.   Any lord myght hym have
   This chyld to his son.

At the door the shepherds pause, struck by a
kindly thought.

Primus Pastor.   Gaf ye the chyld any thyng ?
Secundus Pastor.   I trow not oone farthyng.
Tercius Pastor.   Fast agayne wille I flyng,
   Abyde ye me there.
   Mak, take it to no grefe, if I com to thi
     barne.
Mak.   Nay, thou does me greatt reprefe, and
     fowlle has thou farne.
Tercius Pastor.   The child wille it not grefe, that lytylle
     day starne.

---

[1] except spiders.   [2] tender.   [3] empty.   [4] boy.

Mak, with youre lefe, let me gyf youre
barne,

Bot vj pence.

Mak.   Nay, do away ; he slepys.

Tercius Pastor.   Me thynk he pepys.

Mak.   When he wakyns he wepys.

I pray you go hence.

Tercius Pastor.   Gyf me lefe hym to kys, and lyft up the
      clowtt.

What the deville is this? he has a long
      snowte.

Primus Pastor.   He is markyd amys. We wate ille abowte.

Secundus Pastor.   Ille spon[1] weft, iwis, ay commys foulle owte.

Ay, so?

He is lyke to oure shepe.

Tercius Pastor.   How, Gyb ! may I pepe?

Primus Pastor.   I trow, kynde wille crepe

Where it may not go.

Secundus Pastor.   This was a quantte gawde[2] and a far cast.

It was a hee frawde.

Tercius Pastor.   Yee, syrs, wast.

Lett bren this bawde and bind hir fast.

A fals skawde[3] hang at the last ;

So shalle thou.

Wylle ye se how thay swedylle

His foure feytt in the medylle?

Sagh I never in a credylle

A hornyd lad or now.

Mak.   Peasse byd I : what ! lett be youre fare ;

I am he that hym gatt, and yond woman
      hym bare.

---

[1] spun.   [2] quaint trick.   [3] All false scolds.

Primus Pastor. What deville shall he hatt?
　　　　　　Mak, lo God, Mak's ayre.

Secundus Pastor. Let be alle that. Now God gyf hym care,
　　　　　　I sagh.

Uxor. A pratty child is he
　　　As syttes on a woman's kne ;
　　　A dylle doune, parde,
　　　To gar a man laghe.

Tercius Pastor. I know hym by the eere marke ; that is a
　　　　　　good tokyn.

Mak. I telle you, syrs, hark : hys noys was broken.
　　　Sythen told me a clerk, that he was for-
　　　　　spokyn.[1]

Primus Pastor. This is a false wark. I wold fayne be
　　　　　　wrokyn : Gett[2] wepyn.

Uxor. He was takyn with an elfe :
　　　I saw it myself.
　　　When the clok stroke twelf
　　　Was he forshapyn.

Secundus Pastor. Ye two ar welle feft, sam in a stede.

Tercius Pastor. Syn thay manteyn thare theft, let do thaym
　　　　　　to dede.[3]

Mak. If I trespas eft,[4] gyrd[5] of my heede.
　　　With you wille I be left.

Primus Pastor. Syrs, do my reede.
　　　For this trespas,
　　　We wille nawther ban ne flyte,
　　　Fyght nor chyte,
　　　Bot have done as tyte,
　　　And cast hym in canvas.

---

[1] enchanted.　　　　[2] Collier conjectures Lett = cease.
[3] death.　　　　[4] again.　　　　　　　[5] cut.

The supernatural incidents added to this frank drama of common life have only the slightest thread of connection with the main plot. There is no further burlesque, after Mak has been exposed and tossed in a blanket, except in the persistent attempts of the shepherds to try their cracked voices at the angel song. When they are in the presence of the Holy Child, there is not a trace of intentional irreverence. The stable scene is one of great naiveté, but the shepherds' homely terms of endearment, their simple gifts,—a bird, a ball, a "bob of cherys," and their pleasure when the "swetyng" "merys," and "laghys," are not without tender suggestion of the sanctities of hearth and home.

The next play in order has for theme the coming of the Magi. The central character is Herod, swaggering about fiercely in his blue satin gown and gilded helmet. He is the prince of blusterers, and a devout worshipper of Mahomet. This noisy pageant is succeeded by a quiet night-scene at Bethlehem. Joseph is called from his sleep by an angel

"As blossom bright on bogh,"

and bidden rise and flee. The countrified old carpenter appears, as usual, bewildered and reluctant. It is some time before the angel can make him understand what is wanted of him, and then he protests that he is sick and sore, and his bones ache, and that he doesn't know the way to Egypt. But toward Mary, whose alarm is all for her child, Joseph assumes an air of dignified rebuke, bids her give over her "dyn" and dress the baby and pack up the "gere" at once. What Joseph does is not apparent. Perhaps he saddles the ass. At all events, he finds time to bemoan his lot at length, and warn all young men against matrimony. Then comes a stormy pageant presenting, somewhat absurdly, the slaughter of the Innocents. Three soldiers, at the instigation of the furious Herod, engage in hand to hand combat with three distracted mothers, and, having slain each a child, ride back in triumph to their master, claiming to have killed "many thowsandes." The delighted tyrant, for reward, offers each a fair bride, but they delicately suggest that gold and silver would be more acceptable, and so he promises them a hundred thousand pounds apiece, with castles and towers. Herod then returns thanks to "Mahoune," exults over the thought of the multitude of innocents bloodily murdered, and closes his long address with the unexpected recommendation : —

> "Sirs, this is my counselle,
> Bese not to cruelle,
> Bot adew to the devylle ;
> I can no more Franche."

From this it is a natural inference that Herod, as a socially exalted personage, originally was accustomed, in some or all of his discourses, to use the Norman tongue.

The conclusion of the next Mystery in order, *Purificatio Mariæ*, and the commencement of the following, *Pagina Doctorum*, are lost. Simeon, describing with homely vividness his manifold infirmities of age, prays for a sight, before he dies, of the long-promised Immanuel. Two angels assure him that his prayer is heard in Heaven, and bid him seek the newborn Christ in the Temple. He turns his slow steps thitherward, wondering at the ringing of the bells, and encounters Joseph and Mary on their way to make the offering of turtle-doves. Angel voices call to him to behold the child in Mary's arms, — and here the leaf is torn away.

Pagina Doctorum, suffering from the same mutilation, opens abruptly in the midst of a discussion of the Rabbis, concerning Messianic prophecy. One of them, as he pores over the ancient roll, not unpoetically expands the Hebrew reference to "a root out of Jesse."

Tercius Magister. Masters, youre resons ar right good,
      And wonderfulle to neven,
      Yit fynde I more by Abacuk ;
      Syrs, lysten a whyle unto my steven.[1]

[1] voice.

Our baylle, he says, shalle turn to boytt,
Her afterward som day ;
A wande shalle spryng fro Jessy roytt,
The certan sothe thus can he say.
And of that wande shalle spryng a floure,
That shalle spryng up fulle hight,
Ther of shalle com fulle swete odowre,
And therupon shalle rest and lyght
The Holy Gost, fulle mych of myght,
The Goost of wysdom and of wyt
Shalle beyld his nest, with mekylle right,
And in it brede and sytt.

The child Jesus steps in among the Rabbis with gentle greeting, and is bidden by two of them run away, as they are too busy to be troubled by "barnes"; but the third, the sweeter spirit who had so lovingly dwelt on the old text, calls Jesus to his knee and offers to teach him. The boy quietly protests that he knows as much as they, and when they would test him with questions, excites their wonder and admiration by reciting the ten commandments. At this point Joseph and Mary enter some remote door of the Temple (the mediæval playwright evidently conceiving of the building as a Gothic cathedral), distressfully seeking the lost child, but the sight, afar off, of Jesus among the Rabbis restores their peace. Mary strives in vain to persuade Joseph to go forward and call the boy away, while Joseph, as always, hangs back, abashed by the costly clothes of the Pharisees.

Maria.   Now, dere Joseph, as have ye seylle,[1]
          Go furthe and fetche youre son and myne ;
          This day is goyn nere ilka deylle,
          And we have nede for to go hien.

Josephus. With men of myght can I not melle,[2]
          Then alle my travelle mon I tyne ;[3]
          I can not with thaym, that wote ye welle,
          Thay are so gay in furrys fyne.

Maria.   To thaym youre erand forto say
          Surely that thar ye dred no deylle,
          Thay wille take hede to you alway
          Be cause of eld, this wote I weylle.

Josephus. When I com ther what shalle I say?
          For I wote not, as have I ceylle,[1]
          Bot thou wille have me shamyd for ay,
          For I can nawthere crowke ne knele.

Maria.   Go we togeder, I hold it best,
          Unto yond worthy wyghtes in wede,
          And if I se, as have I rest,
          That ye wille not then must I nede.

Josephus. Go thou and telle thi taylle fyrst,
          Thi son to se[4] wille take good hede ;
          Weynd furthe, Mary, and do thi best,
          I com behynd, as God me spede.

Mary addresses herself to her son, who reminds
her that he must be about his " fader warkys," but,
nevertheless, says a courteous farewell to the Rabbis,
of whom the first two give him praise and good

---

[1] happiness.   [2] mingle.   [3] lose.   [4] thee?

wishes, while the third would have him take up his
abode with them, and accompanies Mary and Joseph
from the Temple. The Madonna's heart brims with
gladness.

> *Maria.* Fulle welle is me this tyde,
>   Now may we make good chere.

But the uncourtly carpenter is only anxious to
be off.

> *Josephus.* No longer wylle we byde.
>   Fare welle alle folk in fere.[1]

The nineteenth pageant, Johannes Baptista, is distinguished among the others by its dull and prosaic
character, and by its jogging metre. John, who introduces himself and his errand to the audience in
the initial speech, is instructed by two angels to bap-
tise Jesus there in the "flume Jordan." He objects,
both as feeling himself unworthy to touch the Lord's
body, and as considering it more reverential that he
should go and meet the Saviour, rather than await
by the riverside Christ's coming. But when the
angels insist that it is better that the Lord should
come to him, John deduces a moral.

> " By this I may welle understand
>   That chylder shuld be broght to kyrk,
>   For to be baptysyd in every land."

---

[1] company.

Later on, too, in the very act of the baptism,

> " In the name of thi Fader fre,
> In nomine Patris et Filii
> Sen he wille that it so be,
> Et Spiritûs altissimi,
> And of the Holy Goost on he,"

John inserts a priestly discourse on the seven sacraments.

> " Here I the anoynt also
> With oyle and creme in this intent,
> That men may wit, where so thay go,
> This is a worthy sacrament.
> Ther ar Vj othere and no mo,
> The whiche thi self to erth has sent,
> And in true tokyn, oone of tho
> The fyrst on the now is it spent."

It is of interest to notice that these lines have been crossed out in the manuscript, the figure Vj altogether erased, and against the passage the words written : " Correctyd and not played." The inference is that the pageant was acted at least once or twice after the Reformation. The rite of baptism concluded, Jesus gives a lamb to John, who remains preaching in the wilderness.

Now comes the third and last group of the Towneley Mysteries, where, however rude the expression, the intent throughout, with the exception of a single scene, is tragic. The representation of the Saviour's

Passion, physically realistic as these primitive play-wrights strove to make it, was doubtless beheld in all devoutness by a hushed, heart-smitten audience. Pilate is the blusterer now, and it is he who takes the lead in the conspiracy against Jesus. The Last Supper is presented, the dialogue adhering closely to the Gospel text. The rhyming is often imperfect, and the diction bald, but here and there occurs a touch of poetry, and the feeling is always reverent and tender.

> " Now loke youre hartes be grefyd noght,
>   Nawther in drede nor in wo,
>   But trow in God, that you has wroght,
>   And in me trow ye also ;
>   In my fader house, for sothe,
>   Is many a wonnyng stede,[1]
>   That men shalle have aftyr thare trowthe,
>   Soyn after thay be dede.
>   And here may I no longer leynd,[2]
>   Bot I shalle go before,
>   And yit if I before you weynd,
>   For you to ordan thore,
>   I shalle com to you agane,
>   And take you to me,
>   That where so ever I am
>   Ye shalle be with me.
>   And I am way and sothe-fastnes,
>   And lyfe that ever shalbe,
>   And to my fader comys none, iwys,
>   Bot oonly thorow me.

[1] dwelling-place.   [2] tarry.

I wille not leyf you all helples,
As men withoutten freynd ;
As faderles and moderles,
Thof alle I fro you weynd ;
I shalle com eft to you agayne,
This warld shalle me not se,
But ye shalle se me welle certan,
And lyfand shalle I be.
And ye shalle lyf in heven,
Then shalle ye knaw lwys,
That I am in my fader even
And my fader in me is."

Later comes the prayer of Gethsemane : —

" Fader, let this great payn be stylle,
And pas away fro me ;
Bot not, fader, at my wylle,
Bot thyn fulfylled be."

After the betrayal come the scenes of the buffet-
ing and scourging, with all the brutality emphasised
and elaborated. These painful effects are continued
throughout the trial scene and the scene in the Via
Dolorosa, while the crucifixion pageant is wellnigh
intolerable. Every detail of the physical torture
is forced into prominence, and the spiritual glory
that, in the Gospel narrative, makes the anguish
of Calvary a "sorrow more beautiful than beauty's
self" is almost utterly wanting. As a relief from
the tragic tension, the casting of lots for the seam-

less vesture is farcically handled, and is followed
by the popular pageant known as the Harrowing
of Hell, which gives the actors who take the devil-
rôles their opportunity. The spirit of Jesus, while
the body still slumbers in the sepulchre, treads the
steep path to hell. As the gleam of light shed
before the steps of the coming deliverer grows
brighter and brighter, the imprisoned souls wax
eager in anticipation, Isaiah, Simeon, John the Baptist, and Moses confirming the new hope. The
demon warders grow restless, and listen fearfully
for the awful voice that soon thunders at their
gates : " Lift up your heads, O ye gates ! And be
ye lifted up, ye everlasting doors ! And the King
of Glory shall come in." After vain parley with the
threatening stranger, Beelzebub calls up Satan, the
Lord of Hell, who ascends in all his terrors, but is
smitten down by the resistless arm of Christ. For
Judas, Cain, and the Roman Cato — poor Cato, who
must need all his philosophy to reconcile him to
such a classification — there is no rescue, but the
other spirits, hand in hand, led by Adam, who is
led by Christ, troop up from the black jaws of hellmouth, singing the Te Deum.

The Resurrection pageant follows with comparative
fidelity the Gospel narrative, although the Saviour,
on emerging from the tomb, utters a long and touch-
ing appeal to the audience, beginning, —

> " Erthly man that I have wroght
> Wightly wake, and slepe thou noght,
> With bytter baylle I have the boght,
>   To make the fre ;
> Into this dongeon depe I soght
>   And alle for luf of the."

He displays his wounds, rehearses his agonies.

> " Sen I for luf, man, boght the dere,
> As thou thi self the sothe sees here,
> I pray the hartely, with good chere,
>   Luf me agane ;
> That it lyked me that I for the
>   Tholyd[1] alle this payn.
> If thou this lyfe in syn have led,
> Mercy to ask be not adred,
> The leste drope I for the bled
>   Myght clens the soyn,
> Alle the syn the warld with in
>   If thou had done."

With outspread arms the white-robed figure yearns toward the tearful listeners.

> " Lo how I hold myn armes on brade,
> The to save ay redy mayde,
> That I great luf to the had,
>   Welle may thou know !
> Som luf agane I wold fulle fayn
>   Thou wold me show.
> Bot luf noghte els aske I of the,

---

[1] suffered.

> And that thou fownde[1] fast syn to fle,
> Pyne the to lyf in charyte
>   Bothe night and day ;
> Then in my blys that never shalle mys
>   Thou shalle dwelle ay."

The fishers of Wakefield set forth the walk to
Emmaus, and the evening meal, the episode of doubt-
ing Thomas follows, and then the ascension pageant.
Doomsday completes the series.   The dead have
just arisen from their graves, sworded angels drive
the greedy demons away from the righteous, while
the cloud-enthroned Christ, with the sound of trump,
descends from heaven for judgment.   The devils
quake before Him, but claim their legitimate prey,
gleefully reading from their books long lists. of
evildoers.   Their harsh tones and harsher laughter
are hushed by the voice of Christ, Who, displaying
His pierced hands and wounded side, tells over once
again the story of His sufferings.

> " Thus was I dight thi sorow to slake,
>   Man, thus behovid the borud[2] to be,
>   In alle my wo tooke I no wrake,[3]
>   My wille it was for luf of the :
>   Man, for sorow aght the to quake,
>   This dredful day this sight to se,
>   Alle this suffred I for thi sake,
>   Say, man, what suffred thou for me ? "

---

[1] try.   [2] ransomed.   [3] vengeance.

To the souls on the right and to the souls on the left their dooms are meted out, and while the demons seize upon their victims, with scoff and threat, the saints sing the Te Deum, and the last pageant-carriage, leaving behind it pale faces and quivering nerves, rolls out of Wakefield market-square and on from street to street until the evening falls.

CHAPTER III.

MIRACLE PLAYS — ENUMERATION.

ENGLISH literature is fortunate in the survival of four of her Mystery cycles, — of five, indeed, if to Cornwall be accorded an English recognition. Yet these are but a portion, and the smaller portion, of Great Britain's original store. The sea of time has an indiscriminate appetite, and swallows, with equal gusto, an Æschylean trilogy and the dramatic patchwork of blundering old monks. A little wreckage from the sunken cycles has been picked up by diligent antiquarians, — the Dublin Abraham play, the Newcastle-on-Tyne Noah play, and by the side of these have drifted ashore other stray pageants with a cyclic suggestion about them, an indefinable air of missing something, like teaspoons that have outworn their set. There are chance notices, too, in out-of-the-way old parchments, of cycles whose manuscripts have long since gone to fatten church-tower rats, and doubtless there were still other cycles, once the boast of goodly towns, that have

left of themselves not the faintest record or tradition.

It is strangest of all that no London cycle has been
preserved. Beside the long and elaborate series
acted there by the parish clerks, the "joly Absolons,"
that dissipated series which required a week and a
day for presentation, there seems to have been a
secondary London group, a three-days' performance,
in addition to a number of isolated pageants pertaining in one way or another to the metropolis. There
was a conspicuous Beverly cycle of thirty-six Corpus
Christi plays, a list of whose titles, nearly corresponding to those of the York series, is extant.
There was a Worcester cycle, probably consisting of
five Corpus Christi plays acted by the guilds. The
old cathedral town of Canterbury, magnet of pilgrims
the kingdom over, was not without its pageant series,
and Heybridge, Preston, Lancaster, and Kendall
appear likewise to have had their own dramatic
versions of the Bible.

Yet deep as is the silence which has fallen on all
that eager bustle of the mediæval English stage, —
on all that stir and pomp and bravery, on the gayly
adorned, emulous pageant-scaffolds rattling hastily
to their posts in the summer dawn, on the rough-
handed players lost in admiration of their own finery,
and rehearsing in every available corner the rant of
Herod, the wail of the Madonna, on the throngs

of spectators crowding to the heads of the narrow streets, delighted to recognise son or sweetheart in gold-plumed angel or white-bearded patriarch, half-shuddering to catch the glance of familiar eyes from under the red tuft of Judas or the black horns of the warder of hellmouth, — still enough remains of tattered, time-yellowed manuscript to enable us to estimate the dramatic significance of this most popular and long-enduring phase that the English drama has ever known.

The cycle most nearly corresponding to the Towneley plays is that of York, probably derived from the same original series, now lost, as this other Northumbrian group, but at an earlier date than the Towneley. The York cycle has another and still closer parallel in that remarkable poem of the Durham district, the *Cursor Mundi*, which, like the York collection of plays, the three other series being less complete, comprehensively sets forth the sacred history from creation to doomsday, and which bears the further resemblance to the York Mysteries of being comparatively free from the element of comedy that enters so largely into the Towneley plays. The Chester cycle, too, abounds in jocular incidents, while the Coventry is quite as grave and decorous as the York.

The York plays were performed within the walls of that stately old city by the craft-guilds on the festival of Corpus Christi in the fourteenth, fifteenth, and sixteenth centuries. This venerable and important cycle was, however, the last of all to make its way into print. Although repeatedly and insistently called for, it was not given to the literary world until 1885, in Miss Lucy Toulmin Smith's edition, an edition so good as to make amends for the delay. The Earl of Ashburnham, so reluctantly yielding up his treasured manuscript to the vulgar press, bought it from a gentleman, who, in 1842, had paid for it £305, though in 1764 it had been bought by Horace Walpole for one guinea. These figures are significant as showing the increased value set, with the increase of knowledge, upon our early English literature. A second illustrious name is connected with the story of this old parchment volume, for it was at one time in the possession of Henry Fairfax, uncle to the Parliamentarian general, Lord Fairfax. This distinguished soldier, in addition to the honour of having a sonnet inscribed to him by Milton, may have had the unconscious glory of saving these plays, as he saved other manuscripts, from destruction, at the blowing up of St. Mary's Tower in York. It is likely enough that this old folio was among the miscellaneous literary deposit of the Tower, though there is no direct proof to be obtained, for of the volume's prior history we know only that it was kept in York under the control of the City Corporation, but in the care — for some of the time, at least — of the priory of Holy Trinity, which shared at the Reformation the general fate of Roman Catholic establishments in England.

The York pageants number forty-eight. Five of these, — the Israelites delivered from Egypt, Christ in the Temple, the Harrowing of Hell, the Resurrection, and the Day of Judgment, — are repeated, sometimes even verbatim, in the Towneley collection. These York plays are usually divided, often with no little dramatic skill, into scenes. One of their most striking features is the variety in metre and stanzaic arrangement they present, the measure often changing with a new speaker or a new emotion.

Sweetly cadenced, for example, is Elizabeth's greeting to Mary.

> " Welcome ! mylde Marie,
>   Myn aughen cosyne so dere,
> Joifull woman am I,
>   þat I nowe see þe here.
> Blissed be þou anely
>   Of all women in feere [1]
> And þe frute of thy body
>   Be blissid ferre and nere."

But the swaggerers, as Herod, run the letter at full gallop.

---

[1] company.

" Dragons þat are dredfull schall derke in þer denne,
    In wrathe when we writhe, or in wrathenesse ar wapped,
Agaynste jeanntis[1] on-gentill have we jŏined with ingen,
    And swannys þat are swymmyng to oure swetnes schall
        be suapped."

The York dramatist usually handles his verse with
ease and often with grace.   It is but rarely that his
rhyme trips him into an absurdity, as when Satan,
in the Temptation scene, is urging Christ to cast
Himself down from the height.

    " For it is wretyn, as wele is kende,
        How God schall anngellis to þe sende,
        And they schall kepe þe in þer hande
                wher-so þou gose,
        þat þou schall on no stones descende
                to hurte þi tose."

The general character of the York cycle is dignified and devout, and yet passages frequently occur
of realistic force and even of vivacity.   The quarrel
between Adam and Eve after the fall is capitally
done.

Adam. To see it is a synfull syghte,
        We bothe þat were in blis so brighte,
        We mon go nakid every-ilke a nyght,
                and dayes by-dene.
        Allas ! what womans witte was light !
                þat was wele sene.

----

[1] giants.

Eue. Sethyn it was so me knyth it sore,
 Bot sythen that woman witteles ware,
 Mans maistrie shulde haue bene more
   agayns þe gilte.

Adam. Nay, at my speche wolde þou never spare,
   þat has vs spilte.

Eue. Iff I hadde spoken youe oughte to spill,
 Ye shulde haue taken gode tent þere tyll,
   and turnyd my þought.

Adam. Do way, woman, and neme it nought,
 For at my biddyng wolde þou not be,
 And therfore my woo wyte y thee [1]
 Thurgh ille counsaille þus casten ar we,
   in bittir bale.
 Now god late never man oftir me
   triste woman tale.

If the York plays seem subdued in tone after the Towneley collection, we must do them the justice to admit that their religious sentiment is deeper and their general treatment of the Biblical history more reverent and appropriate. Yet frequently the conception jars, as in the naïve reason assigned by God for the creation of man, although the second strophe goes far toward redeeming the first and third.

 "This werke is wrought nowe at my wille,
  But yitte can I here no beste see
 That accordes by kyndly skylle [2]
  And for my werke myghte worshippe me.

---

[1] charge I to thee.   [2] natural intelligence.

For parfite werke ne were it none
　But oughte wer made þat myghte it zeme,[1]
For love made I þis worlde alone,
　Therfore my love shalle in it seme.
To keepe this worlde bothe more and lesse
　A skylfull beeste than will y make,
Aftir my shappe and my liknesse,
　The whilke shalle wirshippe to me take."

The Cain pageant, again, is curiously clumsy, ill-timed, and undramatic in its attempts at comedy, — a conspicuous contrast to the natural fun, rude though it is, of the corresponding Towneley play. Cain, for instance, strikes the angel who brings him God's malison, and the messenger, in most uncelestial anger, makes the divine curse heavier by the weight of his own.

The Passion pageants, too, are distressful, presenting a large amount of extra-Scriptural matter and drawing out beyond all endurance the scenes of insult and torture. The characteristic attempt of the English guilds to achieve realism in all the practical details of the presentation, carpentercraft, sailorcraft, and smithcraft, is nowhere more strikingly exhibited than in the crucifixion scenes of the York cycle. But this stress laid on fastening the victim to the cross in a workmanlike manner and wedging the cross firmly into the mortise, while it

---

[1] care for.

imparts a certain physical reality to the situation, effectually distracts the attention from the spiritual and ideal element. And so with the human by-play which, throughout these Passion pageants, is meant to relieve the tragic tension. All the accessory incidents, as the putting to bed and rousing again of Caiaphas and Pilate, and the buying of Calvary locus from the sadly cheated squire, belittle and confuse the main conception. The York cycle, in its zest for amplification in these Passion pageants, draws largely from legend. We have the story, so fully narrated in the apocryphal gospels, of the bowing of the Roman standards in homage to Jesus, despite the efforts of the standard-bearers to hold them upright, and we even have a hint of the fantastic Cornish legend of the consecrated tree, sprung from Adam's grave, built into Solomon's Temple, laid as a bridge over Kedron, and finally shaped into the Saviour's cross :—

> " I have bene garre make
> þis crosse, as yhe may see,
> Of þat laye ouere þe lake,
> Men called it þe kyngis tree."

The Pilate family is prominent in this Passion group, the son being introduced as often as possible, and the wife having a semi-comic part to play. We first find her arousing the displeasure of the

beadle by kissing her husband, and drinking with him
in the Judgment Hall, but after she has gone home
to sleep, the Devil, foreseeing the harrowing of hell,
whispers in her ear and stirs her to an unavailing
effort to save the life of Jesus. Pilate himself is handled with unusual gentleness by the York playwright,
being depicted as fair of person and noble of heart,
but unable to protect his prisoner, to whom he does
involuntary homage, from the hatred of the Jews.

But although the conception often disappoints
and repels, occasionally we are surprised by an
almost subtle touch, as in the lament of the Eden
exiles for the sorrow their sin has brought upon
the innocent earth, a stanza curiously anticipating
that scene in Mrs. Browning's *Drama of Exile*, where
the reproachful spirits of the earth and of the creatures confront the two curse-bringers : —

> "Alas ! for bale, what may this bee?
> In worlde unwisely wrought have wee,
> This erthe it trembelys for this tree,
>   and dyns ilk dele.
> Alle this worlde is wroth with mee,
>   this wote I wele."

Very beautiful is God's loving delight in giving
His blessing, which He bestows over and over, as
upon the conclusion of His creative work.

> "At heuene and erthe firste I be-ganne,
> And vj daies wroughte or y wolde reste,

My werke is endid nowe at manne,
Alle likes me wele, but þis þe beste.
    My blissynge haue they ever and ay ;
    þe seuynte day shal my restyng be,
    þus wille I sese, sothly to say,
    Of my doyng in þis degree.
        To blisse I schal you bringe,
        Comes forthe ȝe two with me,
            ȝe shalle lyff in likyng,
        My blissyng with you be."

Even the creative act, no less than the after ap-
proval, is designated as God's blessing.

"Ande in my fyrste makyng to mustyr my mighte,
    Sen erthe is vayne and voyde, and myrknes emel,[1]
I byd in my blyssyng ȝhe anngels gyf lyghte
    To þe erthe, for it faded when þe fendes fell."

A true touch of spiritual feeling occurs in the
Noah pageant, where the patriarch, five hundred
years old when he goes about his undertaking,
finds with joy and thanksgiving, like Joseph in the
journey to Egypt, that his weakness is made
strength. Nor is Noah's wife as unruly as in the
Towneley series, though she shows pardonable re-
sentment against her husband for having kept his
daily occupation a secret from her all the hundred
years.

"Thow shulde have witte my wille,
    If I wolde sente[2] ther tille.

[1] amidst.   [2] consent.

The attempts of the York dramatist to introduce family strife into the Noah pageant are amusingly perfunctory. Under all the patriarchal bickerings is a fundamental sweetness and serenity of household tone.

The Abraham pageant is out of the common order, there being an effort to ennoble the pathos by a novel conception of Isaac. He is represented as a young man of thirty years, who, on his way to the Mount of Vision, without suspicion of what awaits him there, gives expression to his willingness to yield up his life at God's bidding. The heart-troubled father says wistfully : —

> *Abraham.* Sone, yf oure lord god almyghty
> Of my selfe walde have his offerande,
> I wolde be glade for hym to dye,
> For all oure heele hyngis in his hande.
> *Isaac.* Fadir, for suth, ryght so walde I,
> Lever than lange to leve in lande.
> *Abraham.* A ! sone, thu sais full wele, for thy
> God geve the grace grathely to stande.

Yet the reader is constrained to feel that Isaac's submission, on learning his doom, is unnatural in its composure, although as he lies bound beneath the sword there is wrung from him one bitter cry : —

> " A ! dere fadir, lyff is full swete."

And even the most reverential student of Miracle plays bites back a smile, when the young man, as

they descend the mountain, receives his father's mat-
rimonial decree with the same tranquil resignation
which he had shown upon the altar.

Abraham.   Nowe sone, sen we þus wele hase spede,
    That god has graunted me thy liffe,
    It is my wille þat þou be wedde,
    And welde a woman to thy wyffe ;
    So sall thy sede springe and be spredde,
    In the laweȝ of god be reasoune ryffe.
    I wate in what steede sho is stede,[1]
    That þou sall wedde, withowten stryffe.
    Rabek þat damysell,
    Hir fayrer is none fone,
    The doughter of Batwell,
    That was my brothir sone.
 Isaac.   Fadir, as þou likes my lyffe to spende,
    I sall assente vnto the same.
Abraham.   One of my seruandis sone sall I sende
    Vn-to þat birde to brynge hir hame.

The repentant anguish of Judas, graphically described as the possessor of "a kene face uncomely
to kys," is emphasised; the comic strain in the shepherd scenes is almost lost in the tone of longing
and adoration; the Transfiguration calls forth the
poet's devoutest response of feeling and of fancy,
and throughout the gospel pageants the figure of
Jesus, in however unseemly environment, loses nothing of its gentle majesty. He bows not to Pilate
nor kneels to Herod. The first deals with Him

---

[1] place she abides.

kindly, but Herod, whose heart "hoppis for joie" at the prisoner's advent, expecting "gude game with þis boy," makes huge sport of Christ's silence, shouting at Him as if He were deaf and plying Him with Latin and with French. The soldiers, too, make a jest of the "fool-king," answering even His murmurs from the cross with brutal mockery.

> "We ! harke ! he jangelis like a jay."
> "Me thynke he patris like a py." [1]

>   *   *   *   *   *

> "Yaa, late hym hynge here stille
> And make mowes on the mone." [2]

Akin to the gleams of spiritual discernment in the York plays is the quiet light of homely beauty shed over the domestic scenes. Joseph appears throughout as a lovable rather than ridiculous figure. His evening prayer is very human in its simplicity.

> "Thow maker þat is most of myght,
> To thy mercy I make my mone,
> Lord ! se vnto þin symple wight
> That hase non helpe but þe allone.
> For all þis worlde I haue for-saken,
> And to thy seruice I haue me taken."

On the journey into Egypt, he comforts, protects, and encourages the terrified young mother, bearing the child on his own arm when her slighter arm is

---

[1] chatters like a magpie.   [2] grimaces to the moon.

wearied.   There is a genuinely domestic atmosphere,
by the way, about the hurried preparations for the
flight.   Mary, too much distracted to aid, clasps the
child to her heart, while Joseph busies himself with
the packing, greatly concerned lest something be
forgotten, yet, although grumbling a little under his
breath, ever patient in answering the appeals of his
wife, who shows herself, on this occasion, no stronger
than a woman and no wiser than a girl.

> *Mary.*   Allas ! Joseph, for care !
>   Why shuld I for-go hym,
>   My dere barne þat I bare ?
> *Joseph.* þat swete swayne yf þou saue,
>   Do tyte, pakke same oure gere,
>   And such smale harnes as we haue.
> *Mary.*   A ! leue Joseph, I may not bere.
> *Joseph.* Bere arme ? no, I trowe but small,
>   But god it wote I muste care for all,
>   For bed and bak,
>   And alle þe pakke
>   þat nedis vnto vs.
>
> *   *   *   *   *
>
>   But god graunte grace I noght for-gete
>   No tulles þat we shulde with vs take.
> *Mary.*   Allas ! Joseph, for greuaunce grete !
>   Whan shall my sorowe slake,
>   For I wote noght whedir to fare.
> *Joseph.* To Egipte talde I þe lang are.[1]

[1] long ago.

Mary. Whare standith itt?
    Fayne wolde I witt.

Joseph. What wate I?
    I wote not where it standis.

Mary. Joseph, I aske mersy,
    Helpe me oute of þis lande.

Joseph. Nowe certis, Marie, I wolde full fayne,
    Helpe þe al þat I may.

But loveliest of all is the Nativity pageant, where we find Joseph and Mary taking shelter in a cattle-shed at Bethlehem and enduring the rigours of such Christmas weather as is better known to Yorkshire than to Palestine.

Joseph. A ! lorde, what the wedir is colde !

Mary. þe fellest freese þat euere I felyd,
    I pray God helpe þam þat is alde,
    And namely þam þat is vnwelde.

While Joseph is gone out for light and fuel, Mary, whose heart is uplifted above all consciousness of hardship and of pain, gives birth to the Holy Child, and rejoices over Him with eager and reverent devotion.

Mary. Nowe in my sawle grete joie haue I,
    I am all cladde in comforte clere.

*   *   *   *   *

    Jesu ! my son þat is so dere,
        nowe borne is he.

*   *   *   *   *

> Vowchesaffe, swete sone I pray þe,   .
> That I myght þe take in þe armys of myne,
> And in þis poure wede to arraie þe ;
>   Graunte me þi blisse !
> As I am thy modir chosen to be
> In sothfastnesse.

Joseph, nearing the shed, beholds a sudden light, and enters to find the Child in Mary's arms.

Joseph. O Marie ! what swete thyng is þat on thy kne ?

On realising that the Christ is indeed come to them, Joseph joins Mary in loving adoration. The cattle know their Lord, and low from their stalls, so wistful to render Him service that the parents lift the little sleeper and lay Him softly in the manger, that the beasts may cherish the tender body with their warm breath.

Among the non-Biblical characters of the York cycle are eight burgesses and two porters, the second of these, hard to rouse, and of abusive tongue, belonging to the type of Mystery porters that fathered the porter in *Macbeth*. For even Shakespeare owed so much of a direct debt to these antiquated dramas, while Ben Jonson did not scruple to borrow from them the "roaring devil" which Shakespeare ridicules. The York collection has fourteen pageants after the Crucifixion and eight after the Resurrection, three of these last dealing with the Madonna, her death, her appearance to St. Thomas, and her coronation. The relations between the Mother and Son are lovingly depicted, for in this old York series, over which a fragrance of incense seems to linger, the devotional heart play, the fervours and the tendernesses of mediæval Christianity are especially exemplified.

The Chester cycle has been the subject of much critical discussion, with a view to ascertaining whether it is a translation or an original work. Five manuscripts are in existence, all transcripts made in the end of the sixteenth century or beginning of the seventeenth from a manuscript no longer extant, but which modern scholars are tolerably agreed in believing, on the evidence of language and orthography as exhibited in the transcripts, to be of no earlier date than the fourteenth century. But the tradition that connects the Chester plays with the name of Ralph Higden, a monk of Chester in the fourteenth century, and the laborious author of the *Polychronicon*, has exerted a more or less direct influence upon all discussion of the cycle. Warton, seconded by Malone, suggested that the plays, as they have come down to us, might have been Englished by Higden, under consent of the Pope, from a Latin original now lost. Markland thought there might have been a common Latin source from which both the Chester plays and the French *Mystère du vieil Testament* were taken. Collier broached the theory of direct translation from the French. Marriott assented to Collier. Ulrici admitted the remarkable coincidence of language between the Chester plays and certain French Mysteries, but still held to the possibility of a common Latin source. Ward and Wright leave the question doubtful. Recent German criticism inclines to the French hypothesis.

The Chester plays, like the other Miracles, naturally fell into discredit after the Reformation, but were nevertheless revived from time to time. Yet the prefatory stanzas, known as Banes, delivered upon the representation in June of 1600, reflect an uneasy and apologetic spirit. The pageants, twenty-five in number, beginning on Whit-Monday, required three days for their presentation, and were spiced with jocularity, being allied in this respect to the Towneley cycle rather than to the York or Coventry. The Chester pageant of the Flood is, for instance, one of the most spirited and entertaining of all our English Mysteries. Noah enters upon his task with enthusiasm, and all his household exhibit a most cheerful alacrity in helping the work forward. Shem fetches his axe

" As sharpe as enye in alle this towne."

Ham produces a "hacchatt wounder keeyne," and Japhet flourishes a hammer :—

> " I can make well a pynne,
>   And with this hamer knocke it in."

Even Noah's wife, seconded by her flock of daughters-in-law, promises to lend a hand, provided that not too much is expected of her :—

> " And we shall bringe tymber too,
>   For we mowe nothinge elles doe ;
>   Wemen be weeke to undergoe
>   Anye greate travill."

Shem's wife provides a chopping-block ; Ham's wife collects pitch, and Japhet's wife gathers chips to build a fire for dinner.

The ark is completed with lightning rapidity, but not before Noah's wife has turned perverse. It is all in vain that her husband entreats and commands her to enter. The poor old patriarch finds to his sorrow that the building of the ark was but a trifle compared with the task of getting his wife inside.

> *Noye.* Good wyffe, doe nowe as I thee bydde.
> *Noyes Wiffe.* Be Christe ! not or I see more neede,
>   Though thou stande all daye and stare.
> *Noye.* Lorde, that wemen be crabbed aye,
>   And non are meke I dare well saye ;
>   That is well seene by me to daye,
>   In witnesse of you ichone.

> Good wiffe, lett be all this beare,
> That thou maiste in this place heare ;
> For all the [1] wene that thou arte maister,
> And soe thou arte, by Sante John !

The beasts are driven in, the family take refuge, but still this intractable old lady sits carousing with her cronies over a pot of ale, and refuses to budge an inch for all her husband's entreaties.

Noye.   Wiffe, come in : why standes thou their?
> Thou arte ever frowarde, I dare well sweare ;
> Come in, one Godes halfe ! tyme yt were,
> For feare leste that we drowne.

Noyes Wiff.   Yea, sir, sette up youer saile,
> And rowe fourth with evill haile,
> For withouten fayle
> I will not oute of this toune ;
> But I have my gossippes everyechone,
> One foote further I will not gone :
> The [1] shall not drowne, by Sante John !
> And I maye save ther life.
> The [1] loven me full wel, by Christe !
> But thou lett them into thy cheiste,
> Elles rowe nowe wher thy leiste,
> And gette thee a newe wiffe.

Noye.   Seme, sonne, loe ! thy mother is wrawe ;
> Be God, such another I doe not knowe !

Sem.   Father, I shall fetch her in, I trowe,
> Withoutten anye fayle. —
> Mother, my father after thee sende,
> And byddes thee into yeinder shippe wende.

[1] they.

Loke up and see the wynde,
For we bene readye to sayle.

Noyes Wiffe. Seme, goe againe to hym, and saie ;
I will not come theirin to daye.

Noye. Come in, wiffe, in twentye devilles waye !
Or elles stand their all daye.

Cam. Shall we all feche her in ?

Noye. Yea, sonnes, in Christe blessinge and myne !
I woulde you hied you be tyme,
For of this flude I am in doubte.

The Good Gossippes Songe. The flude comes flittinge in
full faste,
One everye syde that spreades full farre ;
For feare of drowninge I am agaste ;
Good gossippes, lett us drawe nere.
And lett us drinke or we departe,
For ofte tymes we have done soe ;
For att a draughte thou drinkes a quarte,
And soe will I doe or I goe.
Heare is a pottill full of Malmsine good and
stronge ;
Itt will rejoyce bouth harte and tonge ;
Though Noye thinke us never so longe,
Heare we will drinke alike.

While these merry matrons sing their tipsy song
— and a very good song it is, too, for a Mystery
poet to achieve — Noah's sons lift their mother in
their arms and bear her into the ark, where Noah
is so imprudent as to give her greeting : —

"Welckome, wife, into this bote !"

Hereat the indignant dame, the very same who a few hours ago had made the feebleness of woman-kind her excuse for doing as little work as possible, rewards him for his salute with a vigorous cuff.

> " Have that for thy note ! "

And poor Noah, rubbing his ear ruefully, with-draws discomfited : —

> " Ha, ha ! marye, this is hotte !
> It is good for to be stille."

The Nativity play is another marked example of the Chester playwright's turn for fun. Like the cor-responding Towneley pageants, it gives a picture of old-time rural life in northern England, with all its coarseness, its homeliness, and not a little of its rogu-ery and rollick. The first shepherd, Hancken, appears drinking; the second, Harvye, is darning his ragged stocking with a crow's feather; and Tudde, the third, is scouring an old tin pan. They sup together, out in the open fields, off Lancastershire oatcakes, "piggs foote," English black puddings, and other non-Hebraic viands. Their appetites appeased, they blow a horn for the merry lad Trowle, on whom they would bestow the leavings of their feast; but these he rejects with such contempt that a wrestling-bout ensues, in which Trowle successively throws all three. While the shepherds are still caressing their bruises, the star shines out upon them and fills them with affright.

> " What is all this light here
> That shynes so bright here
> On my blacke bearde?
> For to see this sight here
> A man may be afright here,
>   For I am aferde."

But as the heavenly anthem dies away and the
angel fades from view, their fear likewise vanishes,
and they fall to a ridiculous discussion of the Latin
words of the Gloria.

Tercius Pastor. Hit was glore glare with a glee,
Hit was nether more nor lesse.

Trowle. Nay, it was glori, glory, glorious!
Me thoughte that note roune over the
howse:
A semlye man he was and curyous,
But sone awaie he was.

Primus Pastor. Naye, it was glory, glory, with a glo!
And moche of cellsis was therto:
As ever have I reste or roo,
Moche he spake of glasse.

Secundus Pastor. Naye, yt was nether glasse nor glye;
Therfore, fellowe, now stande by.

Tercius Pastor. By my faith! he was some spie,
Our sheepe for to steale.

* * * * *

Secundus Pastor. Nay, be God! it was a gloria,
Sayde Gabrill when he beganne so,
He hade a moche better voyce then I have,
As in heven all other have so.

They conclude by striking up a song more to their comprehension, "Singe troly loly troly loe," and taking the way to Bethlehem. After poking fun at Joseph's bushy white beard and chatting sociably with Mary, they adore the Child, giving him whatever they can spare from about their persons. The little shepherd-boys follow suit, one presenting his bottle, one his hood, one his pipe, and the last his nuthook, so that

> "To pulle doune aples, peares, and plumes,
>   Oulde Joseph shall not nede to hurte his thombes."

The shepherds withdraw in a far more spiritual frame of mind than could have been expected of them. Harvye proposes to turn preacher, Tudde to go beyond the sea as an evangelist, Hancken to roam the desert as a holy pilgrim, and Trowle to take up the yet holier life of an anchorite. They part with kisses and amens.

But in truth this boisterous dramatist of Chester, quaint, mediæval city that it yet is, so quaint and so mediæval that one would hardly be surprised to come upon echoes of the Miracle-Play laughter still reverberating under some arched and carven gateway, can be reverent as well as mirthful. The Bethany pageant and the Last Supper pageant witness how devout his spirit really was. He can be very tender, too, as in the farewell of Isaac, when the boy lies bound upon the altar.

Isaake. Father, greete well my brethren yonge,
　　　And praye my mother of her blessinge.
　　I come noe more under her wynge,
　　　Farewell for ever and aye.
Abraham. Harte, yf thou wouldest borste in three,
　　　Thou shalte never master me ;
　　I will no longer let [1] for thee ;
　　　My God, I maye not greeve.
Isaake. A ! mercye, father, why tarye you soe ?
　　　Smyte of my head and let me goe.
　　I praye ryde me of my woe,
　　　For nowe I take my leve.

The Chester playwright, for all his hearty realism, is not absolutely devoid of the sense of spiritual things, although he sometimes makes an incongruous jumble of the literal and the symbolic. In the Adoration of the Magi, for example, the first king decides to give gold because the look of the place is so mean that the mother must be poor; the second thinks incense might disguise the odours of the stable; and the third presents ointment to assist at the baby's toilet. And yet these offerings find at the same time a deeper interpretation : —

　　" By these geiftes three of good araye,
　　　Three things understande I maie,
　　A kinges power, sooth to saie,
　　　By goulde heare in my hande ;

---

[1] delay.

> And for his godhead lasteth aye,
>   Incense we muste geve hym to daie ;
> And bodelye death also, in good faye,
>   By myrre I understande."

This cycle contains a few unusual pageants, a
Balaam pageant, for one, and an Antichrist pageant, the only English Miracle on that subject
extant, although Germany has a Latin Antichrist
play dating from the reign of the Emperor Bar-
barossa (1152–1190). The Ascension pageant would
seem to indicate that the Chester players were
ingenious in mechanical devices, for the central
scene, where Christ is clothed in blood-red garments and attended by a throng of spirits, takes
place in mid-air. The language here is Latin, and
something of the effect of the old liturgical dramas
is preserved. The Emission of the Holy Ghost, too,
naturally made the leading pageant of this Whitsuntide cycle, is remarkable for aërial no less than
for fiery effects, — two angels, singing responsively
in the upper air, sprinkling flames over the heads of
the apostles. There are certain unique touches of
characterisation in the Chester cycle, as the conception of Cain, who is by disposition gentle and amiable, a fond son, and an enthusiastic farmer : —

> " Mother, for south I tell yt thee,
>   A tylle man I am, and so will I be ;
> As my daddye hath taughte yt me,
>   I will fulfill his lore,"

but given to self-seeking : —

> " Of corne I have greate pleintie,
>   Sacrifice to God, sone shall you see,
>   I will make, to loke yf he
>   Will sende me annye more."

In plot, too, the Chester playwright has devices
of his own, making, for example, one of the slaugh-
tered innocents the son of Herod, who, in the
midst of his reproaches and lamentations, falls a
prey to hideous disease and is borne away by a
demon, this ugly apparition lingering a moment
to warn the company that any man who deals in
Herod's sins may expect to share his fate. The
Chester corps of actors included a comic prologue-
speaker, Gobbet on the Green, and an expositor,
who sat on horseback near the scaffold, and from
time to time threw in explanations for the benefit
of the unlearned. At the close of the Doomsday
pageant, the four Evangelists appeared and recited a
species of epilogue to the entire cycle, to the effect
that, as they had set forth all this history in their
gospels, there was no excuse for men who did amiss.
But the jolly folk of Chester probably cared much
more for another of the distinctive *personæ* of this
series, a loquacious woman whom Chester perhaps
had known as a brewer of adulterated ale and a
dealer in false measures, and who preferred, when

Christ harried hell and led the prisoners forth, to stay behind with her friends the devils.

In addition to the scraps of Latin, which are intended to dignify or sanctify the addresses of God, Christ, and the angels, there is an admixture of French in the speeches of these plays. Those who believe the Chester cycle to have been Englished from a French original consider such passages checked off in the outset by the English pageant master, as superfluous, and so left untranslated. But those who claim that the cycle is originally of English composition observe that the French is used only by the three kings of the east, Octavian and Herod, and hence conclude that the author deemed the court language of Norman England appropriate for royal personages. The verse of this Chester poet is fairly varied, and it is noteworthy that the tormentors speak in the crisp dimeter quatrains, which later, being adopted by Skelton, became known as the Skeltonian stanza : —

> " In woe he is wounden,
>   And his grave is gronden ;
>   No lade unto London
>   Suche lawe can hym lere." [1]

Crude as all this Miracle verse is, a few lines from the Chester plays lodge themselves in memory, as the troubled words of Thomas : —

[1] teach.

> " A mistye thinge it is to me
>   To have beleffe it shoulde so be,"

or the sigh of the lonely disciples : —

> " Peradventure God will shewe us grace
>   To se our Lorde in littill space,
>   And comforted for to be,"

or the simple benediction : —

> " Christ geve you grace to take the waie
>   Unto the joye that lasteth aye."

And there is force of tragic passion in the bitter outcry of the queen, who is found at Doomsday on the left hand of Christ, among her companions in that darkness being, such was the audacity of our Chester playwright, a pope of Rome.

The plays going by the name of the Coventry Mysteries are not clearly proven to be the ones which were played at Coventry. That this steepled town was famous for its Corpus Christi pageants is well known. It is recorded that in 1416 Henry V. went to see them, Queen Margaret in 1456, Richard III. in 1484, Henry VII. in 1486, and Henry VII. with his queen in 1492. On this last occasion the plays are mentioned as the plays of the Grey Friars. Of all these royal visits the most interesting notice extant concerns Queen Margaret's, — a notice occurring in the manuscript annals of Coventry: "On Corpus Christi yeven at nyght came the quene from

Kelyngworth to Coventry, at which tyme she wold not be met, but came privily to se the play there on the morowe, and she sygh then alle the pagentes pleyde save domes day, which might not be pleyde for lak of day, and she was loged at Richard Wodes the groc'r."

Besides these records, we have the often-quoted passage from Heywood's *Interlude of the Four PP :* —

> " For as good happe wolde have it chaunce,
>   Thys devyll and I were of olde acqueyntaunce ;
>   For oft, in the play of Corpus Christi,
>   He hath played the devyll at Coventry."

It is evident, then, that Coventry had a widespread reputation for Corpus Christi plays. But by whom were these plays performed ? By the craft-guilds, as at Wakefield, York, and Chester ? Or by the Grey Friars, whose pageants Henry VII. took his queen to see so near the close of the fifteenth century ? And is this unique quarto manuscript, dated 1468, in the Cottonian library of the British Museum, a collection of Coventry plays at all, or is the title a misnomer ? On the fly-leaf of the manuscript, in the handwriting of Dr. Richard James, librarian to Sir Robert Cotton, appears the following inscription : " Contenta Novi Testamenti scenice expressa et actitata olim per monachos sive fratres mendicantes : vulgo dicitur hic liber Ludus Coventriae, sive Ludus Corporis Christi : scribitur metris Anglicanis."

This volume does not contain the Corpus Christi plays acted by the Coventry guilds. Such plays there were, but the guild account-books and what little survives of the pageant text establish the fact that the guild plays were other than these. Are the plays of the manuscript, then, plays acted at Coventry by the Grey Friars? Would the same town have maintained two cycles of Mysteries — one performed by the trades and one by the friars? There is significance, too, in the concluding lines of the prologue or proclamation, cried through the streets a few days in advance of the time fixed for the representation of the play by heralds who, as they went, waved banners inscribed with sacred emblems : —

> " A Sunday next, yf that we may,
>   At vj of the belle we gynne oure play,
>   In N. (omen) towne, wherfore we pray,
>   That God now be youre spede."

Does not this savour more of a strolling company of actors than of a body of friars resident in Coventry? Yet Coventry friars might sometimes have consented to play in neighbouring towns, and the general character of the plays points more directly than usual to ecclesiastical authorship. So high an authority as Ten Brink, however, although inclined to believe that Coventry witnessed a dramatic rivalry

between the Guilds and the Franciscans, assigns
this so-called Coventry collection to the north-east
of the Midlands, where the internal evidence, both
literary and linguistic, would seem to place it. At
all events, we have here a valuable cycle of Mysteries apparently independent of the York and
Towneley groups, or their common original, if such
they had, on the one hand, and of the Chester
group on the other.

The three most striking features of the Coventry
series are the sobriety of treatment, amounting to
dullness, the pronounced Mariolatry, and the fore-
shadowing of the Moralities by the introduction of
abstract characters. The versification is monotonous, and poetic magic almost altogether wanting,
although the lament of the Madonna is not without a touch of tragic power.

> "A ! A ! A ! how myn hert is colde !
>   A ! hert hard as ston, how mayst thou lest ?
> Whan these sorweful tydynges are the told,
>   So wold to God, hert, that thou mytyst brest.
> A ! Jhesu ! Jhesu ! Jhesu ! Jhesu !
>   Why xuld ye sofere this trybulacyon and advercyté ?
> How may thei fynd in here hertys yow to pursewe,
>   That nevyr trespacyd in no maner degré ?
> For nevyr thyng but that was good thowth ye,
>   Wherfore than xuld ye sofer this gret peyn ?
> I suppoce veryly it is for the tresspace of me,
>   And I wyst that myn hert xuld cleve on tweyn."

It will be noticed that here, as in the Chester plays, in contradistinction from the York and Towneley, the dialogue is seldom allowed to break in upon the regular succession of complete stanzas. The pageants are forty-two in number, of which seven only are concerned with the Old Testament, carrying the familiar story forward in careful verse, plain manner, and decorous tone. Even Cain is respectful, and when Adam bids him go with Abel to sacrifice, utters no further remonstrance than

> " I had levyr gon hom welle ffor to dyne."

It is true that he lays his poorest sheaf upon the altar, but he has a reason for it : —

> " What were God the better, thou sey me tylle,
> To yeven hym awey my best sheff,
> And kepe myself the wers ?
> He wylle neyther ete nor drynke,
> ffor he doth neyther swete nor swynke."

Noah's wife, too, is a disappointingly pious, loving, and well-conducted woman, who enters the ark with thanksgiving. Into this pageant is introduced a curious episode, — blind Lamech with his broad arrow shooting Cain, who, lurking in the bushes, was mistaken for a wild beast by Lamech's youthful guide. The old archer, discovering what he has done, and remembering God's curse on the slayer of Cain, in fury raises his bow and beats out the brains of the poor lad who guided his aim amiss. A Latin hymn is sung by the family in the ark, this series, indeed, being remarkable for the number of chants interspersed with the dialogue. The play of *Abraham and Isaac* affords no relief in this colourless Coventry treatment. Abraham vents the conventional lamentations, but without the fierce conflict of emotions that is at least hinted in the other cycles, and Isaac is a painful little prig.

> *Ysaac.* ffadyr, fyre and wood here is plenté,
>   But I kan se no sacryfice ;
>   What ye xulde offre fain wold I se,
>   That it were don at the best avyse.

The two concluding Old Testament pageants savour more of the pulpit than the stage. In one Moses expounds the Ten Commandments, and in the other the Hebrew kings and prophets set forth the genealogy of Christ.

The Gospel pageants, though scarcely more spirited, have the interest of fresh material in connection with the Virgin Mary, who first appears, a child of three years, dressed in white, being conducted by her parents to the Temple. The high priest is charmed with her sweet looks and with the remarkable facility with which she recites and expounds the fifteen psalms, which are the fifteen degrees from Babylon to Jerusalem. No wonder he exclaims, when the child's voice finally ceases, that it is "an hey meracle." More conversation of devotional tenor follows and a throng of "blyssyd maydens," bearing the names of various virtues, are presented to Mary as her companions and attendants. Joachim and Anna return home, Mary prays before the altar, and an angel "bryngyth manna in a coupe of gold lyke to confeccions," pronouncing an anagram on the name *Maria.* Another angel brings more gifts, and an additional present is sent by the bishop. But the little girl in the white frock bestows these treasures upon the needy, showing already a merciful heart toward the poor : —

> " Pore ffolk ffaryn God knowyth how,
>   On hem evyr I have grett pety."

An interval of ten years is supposed to pass before the events recorded in the next pageant, *Mary's Betrothment,* which discloses all the bachelors in the line of David, summoned by the Bishop, standing in the Temple bearing peeled white rods. The rod of the old Joseph flowers, thus designating him, much to his discomfiture, as Mary's husband. In connection with the backward behaviour of Joseph on this occasion, even the grave poet of the *Ludus Coventriæ* cannot resist a passing smile.

> *Joseph.* A ! shuld I have here? ye lese my lyff:
>   Alas ! dere God, xuld I now rave?
>   An old man may nevyr thriff
>   With a yonge wyff, so God me save !

The lame old bridegroom is obliged to hobble to the altar, but continues his protests even there. Joseph's actions, however, are better than his words. As Mary is to take three attendant maidens with her, the poor carpenter, after hiring for this unexpected family a "lytyl praty hous" at Nazareth, goes away for the next nine months to labour

> " in fere countre,
> With trewthe to maynteyn our housholde so."

In conformity with the general tendency of this cycle, the pageant describing the ascension of Mary is seven times as long as that describing the ascension of Christ. Miracles are wrought about her bier, and her soul is crowned by Christ

> " Queen of Hefne and Moder of Mercy,"

the archangel Michael announcing : —

> " Hefne and erthe in joye may be,
> ffor God throw Mary is mad mannys frend."

The Morality element, too, in these *Ludus Coventriæ,* while marking them as a late cycle, is acceptable to the reader in that it makes for novelty.

Contemplation is a conspicuous figure, speaking prologues and epilogues, acting as expositor, and bearing a part in that heavenly scene where the Father, Son, and Holy Ghost, with various personified qualities, hold council together. We are here very close upon the Moralities, as we see Mercy and Truth meeting, and Justice and Peace kissing each other. Mors, too, a grisly personage well known to the Morality stage, appears at Herod's feast, standing behind the seat of the tyrant who, all unaware of that menacing shadow, urges on the revelry. After Mors has smitten down the cruel king and his two murderous knights, another famous Morality character, the Devil, has a part to play, seizing upon these sinful souls with the grim jest : —

> " Alle oure ! alle oure ! this catel is myn !
>   I zalle hem brynge onto my celle !
> I xal hem teche pleys fyn,
>   And shewe suche myrthe as is in helle ! "

The Devil takes much more upon him in the Coventry series than in any of the earlier cycles. As a prologue to the council of the Jews, he delivers a long harangue, containing some striking passages of dramatic satire, perhaps the earliest in English literature, directed against the fopperies of the day. He lurks in the background of the Last Supper, exulting when Judas rises and goes

out into the darkness.   He whispers a dream into
the sleeping ear of Pilate's wife, and while Jesus
is being reclothed on the scaffold after the scourging, Satan enters "in the most orryble wyse" on
the ground below, and proceeds to divert the audience with buffoonery.   He has little opportunity,
however, to win plaudits in the *Harrowing of Hell*,
as in the Coventry cycle this pageant is apparently short, although there may have been more
in the way of dumb-show than appears from the
text.

Apart from the Mariolatry and Morality features,
these Gospel pageants present little of note.   The
fourteenth play is unique among the Mysteries,
being a rugged, vigorous description, with coarse
jests and sly, satiric touches, of an ecclesiastical
court.

In this fourteenth pageant the Sompnour opens
proceedings with a genuine bit of comic rhyme,
hardly Hebraic in suggestion, but calculated, if
well bawled, to rouse huge mirth in an audience
whose ears would not only be tickled by the rough-
and-ready alliteration, but would often be greeted
in the medley by the sound of a familiar name, —
that of some rustic, whose startled, sheepish looks
would enhance the mirth of his neighbours.

> " Avoyd, seres, and lete my lorde the buschop come,
>   And syt in the courte the lawes ffor to doo ;

And I xal gon in this place them for to somowne,
  Tho that ben in my book the court ye must com too.
    I warne you here alle abowte,
    That I somown you alle the rowte,
    Loke ye fayl, for no dowte,
        At the court to pere.
    Bothe John Jurdon, and Geffrey Gyle,
    Malkyn Mylkedoke, and fayr Mabyle,
    Stevyn Sturdy, and Jak at the Style,
        And Sawdyr Sadelere.

  " Thom Tynkere and Betrys Belle,
    Peyrs Potter and Whatt at the Welle,
    Symme Smalfeyth and Kate Kelle,
        And Bertylmen the Bochere.
    Kytt Cakelere and Colett Crane,
    Gylle Fetyse and fayr Jane,
    Powle Pewterere and Pernel Prane,
        And Phelypp the good Flecchere.

  " Cok Crane and Davy Drydust,
    Luce Lyere and Letyce Lytyltrust,
    Miles the Myllere and Colle Crakecrust,
        Bothe Bette the Bakere, and Robyn Rede.
    And loke ye rynge wele in your purs,
    ffor ellys your cawse may spede the wurs,
    Thow that ye slynge Goddys curs
        Evyn at myn hede, ffast com away.
    Bothe Bontyng the Browstere, and Sybyly Slynge,
    Megge Merywedyr and Sabyn Sprynge,
    Tyffany Twynkelere, ffayle ffor nothynge,
        The courte xal be this day."

The shepherd pageant has no comic features.
The play opens with the angel-song. The shepherds
listen, recite Messianic prophecies, and are guided by
the star to the manger, where they adore the Child in
verse which rises much above the level of the ordi-
nary jog-trot stanza of this cycle. The Magi pageant,
too, is distinguished by the lightness of its cadences,
as well as by a remarkably fine Herod with an extraordinary penchant, which the Devil shares, for alliteration. The mockery of Jesus is by no means given the
prominence or the jocular variety that it had in the
earlier cycles. In the Resurrection pageant, the soldiers, overcome with sleep, confide the care of the
tomb to Mahomet. The short, abrupt stanzas seem to
correspond to the sudden nods of their drowsy heads.

> *Primus miles.* Myn heed dullyth,
>   Myn herte ffullyth
>   Of sslepp.
>   Seynt Mahownd
>   This beryenge ground
>   Thou kepp !
> *Secundus miles.* I sey the same,
>   ffor any blame,
>   I falle.
>   Mahownd whelpe,
>   Aftyr thin helpe
>   I calle !
> *Tertius miles.* I am hevy as leed,
>   ffor any dred
>   I slepe.

> Mahownd of myght
> This ston to nyght
> Thou kepe !

Before leaving the Coventry plays, it should be said that there is some reason to suppose that the Passion pageants of this manuscript belong to a different cycle altogether. They are opened by a sacred procession, whose various personages, Father, Son, Holy Ghost, the twelve apostles, Paul, and John the Baptist are made known to the audience by antiphonal stanzas delivered by two doctors. When Herod, who may have been also a figure in the procession, has taken his scaffold, "and Pylat and Annas and Cayphas here schaffaldys," Contemplation speaks a prologue to this new series.

Of the Corpus Christi pageants acted by the guilds of Coventry something can be learned through their old account-books and their two surviving plays, a *Purification of the Virgin*, acted by the Weavers, and a rambling, mutilated Christmas Mystery, acted by the Barbers and Tailors. These are of little dramatic merit, but an appendix contains words and music for three not untuneful songs, which really reduce themselves to two, the Shepherds' Song and the Song of the Bethlehem Mothers. The Shepherds' Song runs as follows : —

> " As I out rode this enderes [1] night,
> Of thre joli sheppardes I saw a sight ;

[1] last.

And all a bowte there fold, a stare shone bright ;
They sange terli terlowe,
So mereli the sheppardes there pipes can blow.

" Doune from heaven, from heaven so hie,
Of angeles ther came a great com'panie,
With mirthe and joy and great solemnitye ;
The sange terly terlow,
So mereli the sheppards ther pipes can blow."

The other seems to have been sung as solo and
chorus.

" O sisters too,[1] how may we do,
    For to preserve this day,
This pore yongling, for whom we do singe
    By by, lully, lullay.
        Lully, lulla, yow littell tine childe,
            By by, lully, lullay, yow littell tyne child,
                By by, lully, lullay.

" Herod the king, in his raging,
    Chargid he hath this day ;
His men of might, in his owne sight,
    All yonge children to slay.   (*Cho.*)

" That wo is me, pore child, for thee,
    And ever morne and say ;
For thi parting, nether say nor singe,
    By by, lully, lullay."   (*Cho.*)

Allusion should be made to one other Coventry
pageant, — the old Hox Tuesday Play, an annual

---

[1] two.

performance of ancient date in memory of a tradi-
tional victory gained by the good citizens of Coventry and their neighbours over the Danes in 1002.
The derivation of this word Hox is disputed, but
the pageant appears to have been a mimicry of
battle.

Cornwall has a fourteenth-century cycle of Corpus
Christi pageants. These plays, written in Cornish,
are highly valued by philologists as constituting the
most important relic known to exist of the Keltic
dialect as once spoken in Cornwall. Of their literary value it is difficult to judge through the medium
of translation, but they are evidently distinguished
by an absence of the comic element, a great liking
for argumentation, and free play of the wild and
symbolic Keltic imagination. In general scope they
correspond with the English Miracle Cycles, for
although but three main titles are given in connection with this series, *Origo Mundi*, *Passio Domini
Nostri*, and *Resurrexio Domini Nostri*, the Cornwall
plays in reality fill two octavo volumes, follow a
long sweep of Scriptural history, and occupied three
days in the presentation. *Origo Mundi* was given
on the first day, and although the story flows on
without breaks, this play actually embraces, first,
The Temptation and Fall, in which the earth is
made to cry out, as the cursed and exiled Adam
strives to dig, nor will the soil cease resisting and

lamenting, until God comes down from heaven with rebuke; second, *Cain and Abel*, in which the body of poor Abel is dragged off the stage by Beelzebub and Satan; third, *The Birth of Seth;* fourth, *The Death of Adam*, including the legend of Seth's journey to Paradise to beg the oil of heavenly mercy for his father, who is about to die, and content to die, for

> "Strong are the roots of the briars,
> That my arms are broken,
> Tearing up many of them,"

— a journey successful in that a cherub shows Seth the Tree of Life in Paradise, a tree lofty with many boughs, but bare and leafless, with roots piercing down to hell and branches growing high to heaven, with an ugly serpent coiled about the trunk and a new-born child in swaddling clothes shining in the summit, this child the oil of mercy for Adam and all his sons, — a journey from which Seth brings back three seeds of the apple Adam bit, and, by command of the cherub, lays them on his dead father's tongue and presently beholds three rods spring from the grave; fifth, *Noah*, his wife being gentle and obedient, and the scene laid largely in the ark and on Mount Ararat; sixth, *Abraham;* seventh, *Moses and Pharaoh*, carrying the story far on into the experiences of the wilderness, and con-

cluding with the death of Moses, who, just before
yielding up his spirit into the hands of God, plants
again on Mount Tabor the three bright, miracle-
working rods which he had found growing in the
desert; eighth, *David*, who, bidden of Gabriel in a
dream, journeys to Mount Tabor on his yellow
courser and finds there the rods of grace, growing
green and of marvellous fragrance, which he cuts and
brings to Jerusalem, and would have planted there
that they might be ready at need to fashion the
cross of the Son of Man, but in the one night that
King David left them lying, under guard, on the
fair turf, the three rods planted themselves, and by
morning were united into one, an emblem of the
divine Unity in Trinity; ninth, *Bathsheba*, the old,
tragic history; tenth, *Solomon*, who rewards his
workmen with various Cornish parishes for their
exertions in building the Temple, and makes his
favourite councillor first bishop; and eleventh, *Maxi-
milla*, earliest of the Christian martyrs, a maiden
who, having come into the Temple, where one beam,
with which no other wood can be made to correspond, is wrought of the sacred tree, and having
seated herself (somewhat indiscreetly, it would appear) upon a stove, calls upon the Lord Jesus
Christ to extinguish her burning garments, and on
the contemptuous rebuke of the bishop, who has
never heard that name, expounds the mystery of

Trinity and foretells that Christ shall be born of a virgin, a saying for which she is brutally stoned and buffeted to death by order of the bishop, who commands the executioners further to cast out from the Temple the sacred beam, which, heavy on their shoulders and working miracles all the way, is finally thrown as a bridge over the water of Kedron.

With *Passio Domini*, the theme of the second day, comes a change of handwriting, and a marked change of tone, due largely, no doubt, to the nature of the subject. The play of fancy is severely curtailed, and but few legends are allowed to mingle with the Scriptural narrative. There is dignity, but not great power or pathos, in the treatment of the central figure. The violence and coarse brutality of the soldiers are elaborated, as is also the smithcraft of the Crucifixion. In case of several of the lower characters, there are passing touches of comedy. The play does not embrace the birth and childhood of our Lord, but opens with the temptation in the wilderness, Christ being attended by His disciples. The action then moves on through the scenes of Passion Week, — the entry into Jerusalem, Christ giving His blessing to the children who scatter palms before Him and sing Hosanna; the cleansing of the Temple, Pilate, who has come in to pray to Jupiter, being annoyed by the interruption to the fair; the healing of the man

born blind, Pilate and Caiaphas standing by; the
supper at the house of Simon the Leper, with
Iscariot's wrath over the waste of ointment; the
bargain of Judas with Caiaphas, who is attended
by a voluble crozier-bearer; the Last Supper; the
agony in Gethsemane; the betrayal; the denial; the
ecclesiastical trials before Annas and Caiaphas;
the despair and suicide of Judas, whose soul will
not, after the manner of souls, escape through his
mouth, because by a kiss he had betrayed his
Master; the secular trials before Pilate and Herod
and Pilate again; the warning given by Beelzebub
to Pilate's wife in a dream; Pilate's efforts to rescue
Christ; the scourging and the mocking; further
delay of Pilate; the sulky refusals of the jailer
Sharpwhip to bring out his prisoners; much argument by the learned Doctors; the condemnation;
the fashioning a cross of the sacred beam brought
from Kedron; the Via Dolorosa; the unwillingness
of the Christian smith, angrily berated therefor by
his wife, to make the spikes for nailing his Master
to the cross; the Crucifixion; the lament of Mary;
the death of Jesus; the dismay of Lucifer; the descent from the cross, the embalming and the burial.

The third day's play, *Resurrexio Domini Nostri*,
sets forth the imprisonment under nine keys of
Nicodemus and Joseph, that they may not steal
away the body of their Master; the harrowing of

hell, one plucky demon proposing to die in making
up the fire under the kettle wherein he has

> " More than a million souls,
>   In a very fair broth ; "

the rescue, by the Spirit of Christ, of hell's prisoners, sent to Paradise under Michael's escort ; the
Spirit's return to the sepulchre with a company
of angels ; the Resurrection of Christ in the body ;
His appearance to the Madonna ; the report to
Pilate of the sleep-overpowered soldiers, who, stung
by the governor's reproaches, ask after the safety
of his prisoners Joseph and Nicodemus, thus found
to have escaped ; the arrival of the three Marys at
the sepulchre ; Christ's appearance to Mary Magdalene ; her message to the disciples ; a long argument
of Mary and the ten with the unbelieving Thomas ;
the journey to Emmaus ; renewed and greatly prolonged discussion with Thomas, and his final per-
suasion of the truth of the Resurrection. Then
comes a tissue of legends relating to Pilate, on
whom the odium of the Crucifixion is made to rest.
Tiberius Cæsar sends to Pilate for the celebrated
leech, Jesus of Nazareth, to heal him of his leprosy.
There returns to Cæsar a messenger from Veronica,
bearing her sacred handkerchief, the *Veronique*,
which works a miraculous cure on the Roman
Emperor. In gratitude he consents to Veronica's

urgency and orders the execution of Pilate, but the gracious influence of the seamless vesture, now possessed and worn by Pilate, protects the criminal. The robe is removed by force, and Pilate, despairing, stabs himself in the heart; but even then may with difficulty be disposed of, for the earth violently rejects his body, which comes bounding up again as soon as ever it is buried, and which, though enclosed in an iron box, stains the waters of the Tiber black, until at last a rock in the sea splits open and the devils receive Pilate to themselves. The play closes with the Ascension of Christ from His weeping company of followers on earth to the hosts of heaven, where He is beset with questions from nine most inquisitive angels. The Emperor speaks the prologue, succinctly reviewing the sacred history and ending with the words : —

> " Now minstrels, pipe diligently,
> That we may go to dance."

An ancient Cornish poem, entitled *The Passion*, — a poem of over a thousand lines, covering the period from the temptation through the Resurrection, — holds the same relation to the Cornish series of Passion pageants that *Cursor Mundi* holds to the English Miracle Cycles.

The Cornish plays were acted in circular or semicircular stone enclosures, with stone benches or seats of turf for the spectators. Traces of these mediæval theatres are still to be seen in Cornwall.

Of the Dublin cycle the text of one pageant only remains, an *Abraham and Isaac*, performed by the Weavers. This is a surprisingly fresh treatment of the familiar story, standing alone among the six extant Miracles upon this theme in its introduction of Sara among the *dramatis personæ*. Her continual anxiety for Isaac appears even in her farewell words to her husband : —

> "All thing is redy, I you say ;
> But, gentil hert, I you pray,
> Tarry as litel while out as ye may,
> Be cause of Isaac, my sonn."

On learning his doom, the boy's first question is whether his mother knows of it. Abraham answers : —

> "She? nay son, Crist for bede.
> Nay, to telle her it is no nede,
> For whan that ever she knoweth this dede,
> She wol ete affter but litel brede."

And this play, instead of concluding, like the others, on the mountain-top or at its foot, swings about the entire circle and has the final scene at home, where the story is related to Sara, who clasps her recovered child, while the patriarch turns toward the audience to enforce the moral : —

> " Now ye that have sene this aray,
> I warne you all, bothe nyght and day,
> What God comanndeth say not nay,
> For ye shal not lese therby."

Newcastle-on-Tyne had once a series of sixteen plays, from which a solitary *Noah's Ark* has floated down the flood of years. This is an especially absurd version, brief, abrupt, and original. God sends an angel to bid Noah build the ark. Noah, awakened out of sound sleep, greets the angel peevishly:—

> " What art thou for Heaven's King,
> That wakens Noah off his sleeping?
> Away I would thou wend."

Noah's ill-humour is by no means lessened when he understands what a task lies before him. He objects that he is six hundred winters old and with no knowledge of boat-building.

> " Christ be the shaper of this ship,
> For a ship need make I must,"

he groans, and sets about the work.

Then the Devil appears, announcing his intention to have an interview on this business with his friend, Noah's wife. At first she receives his warning against Noah and the ark with rebuke.

> " Go devel, how say, for shame."

But the Devil insists.

> " I swear thee by my crooked snout,
>   All that thy husband goes about
>   Is little for thy profit."

As a result of the Devil's suggestion, Noah's wife, when at evening the old man comes in weary from his work, plies him with drink, learns his secret, and then upbraids him furiously.

> " Who devil made thee a wright,
>   God give him evil to fare.
>
> *   *   *   *   *
>
> The devil of hell thee speed,
>   To ship when thou shalt go."

Noah calls on God for help, and an angel comes to his rescue, whereupon the pageant precipitately ends with an address to the audience from the Devil.

> " All that is gathered in this stead,
>   And will not believe in me,
>   I pray to Dolphin prince of dead,
>   Scald you all in his lead [1]
>   That never a one of you thrive nor thee." [2]

Before leaving the subject of Miracle Cycles for that of isolated pageants, notice should be taken of two curious dramatic productions once pertaining to

[1] chaldron.   [2] prosper.

York, the *Play of Our Lord's Prayer* and the *Creed Play.* The first of these was a favourite with the city, a guild of men and women being formed for the express purpose of keeping it up. Their play-book can be traced down to 1572, when it passed into the hands of the Archbishop of York, and reappeared no more. Apparently it was rather a Morality than a Mystery, holding up the virtues to praise and the vices to scorn. It seems to have had several pageants to correspond with the several clauses of the *Paternoster.* Its date is undiscovered, but Wyclif, who died in 1384, knew of it. In advocating a vernacular translation of the Bible, he refers to "þe paternoster in engliȝsch tunge, as men seyen in þe pley of York." The *Creed Play* had also a guild of its own, and may have been constructed upon much the same plan as the other, which was probably the predecessor; but this play, too, is lost.

Where references exist to the representation of isolated pageants in old English towns, there is room for the presumption that such pageants were but leaves from the cyclic play-book. Where we have, as in a few instances, the text of these fragments, the presumption is usually strengthened.

Norfolk has an *Abraham and Isaac,* the sixth English play on that subject known to be extant. The name appears, too, in the list of plays performed at Beverly and Newcastle-on-Tyne. This is the longest of the six, and excels the other versions in liveliness of dialogue, truthful touches of child-nature, and varied play of parental and devout emotions.

Abraham. Now ysaac, my owyne son dere,
　　　　Wer art thow, chyld? Speke to me.

Ysaac. My fader, swet fader, I am here,
　　　　And make my preyrys to the trenyte.

Abraham. Rysse up, my chyld, and fast cum heder,
　　　　My gentyll barn that art so wysse,
　　　　For we to, chyld, must goo togeder,
　　　　And on-to my lord make sacryffyce.

Ysaac. I am full redy, my fader, loo !
　　　　Yevyn at yowr handes I stand ryght here,
　　　　And wat so ever ye bid me doo,
　　　　Yt schall be don with glad cher,
　　　　　Full wyll and fyne.

Abraham. A ! ysaac, my owyn son soo dere,
　　　　Godes blyssyng I yffe thee and myn.
　　　　Hold thys fagot up on thi bake,
　　　　And her my selffe fyer schall bryng.

Ysaac. Fader all thys here wyll I packe,
　　　　I am full fayn to do yowr bedyng.

Abraham. A ! lord of hevyn, my handes I wryng,
　　　　Thys chyldes wordes all to wond my harte.
　　　　Now ysaac, son, goo we owr wey
　　　　On to yon mounte, with all owr mayn.

Ysaac. Gowe my dere fader as fast as I may,
　　　　To folow you I am full fayn,
　　　　　All thow I be slendyr.

Abraham. A ! lord ! my hart brekyth on tweyn,
   Thys chyldes wordes, they be so tender.

   *   *   *   *   *

Ysaac. Ya ! fader, but my hart begynnyth to quake,
   To se that scharpe sword in yowr hond.
   Wy bere ye yowr sword drawyn soo?
   Off yowre conwnanns[1] I have mych wonder.

Abraham. A ! fader of hevyn, so I am noo !
   Thys chyld her brekys my harte on too.

Ysaac. Tell me, my dere fader, or that ye ses,
   Ber ye yowr sword draw for me?

Abraham. A ! ysaac, swet son, pes ! pes !
   For i-wys thou breke my harte on thre.

Ysaac. Now trewly sum-wat, fader, ye thynke,
   That ye morne thus more and more.

Abraham. A ! lord of hevyn, thy grace let synke,
   For my hart wos never halffe so sore.

Ysaac. I preye yow, fader, that ye wyll let me that wyt,
   Wyther schall I have ony harme or noo?

Abraham. I-wys, swet son, I may not tell the zyt,
   My hart ys now soo full of woo.

On hearing at last the doom in store, Isaac, although he submits, unwilling that his father should incur God's displeasure on his account, yet makes such piteous lament that Abraham strives to silence him.

Abraham. Sone, thy wordes make me to wepe full sore,
   Now my dere son ysaac, speke no more.

[1] countenance.

Ysaac. A ! my owyne dere fader, were fore ?
　　　　We schall speke to-gedyr her but a wylle
　　　　And sythyn that I must nedysse be ded,
　　　　　zyt my dere fader, to you I prey,
　　　　Smythe but feve strokes at my hed,
　　　　　And make an end as sone as ye may,
　　　　　　And tery not too longe.

Yet the father's heart fails him at every effort,
and the bright sword, the sight of which so terri-
fies the boy, swerves again and again from the
fall. Even after the angel has intervened, Isaac,
dazed with fright, can with difficulty be brought
to comprehend his deliverance, and through the
rest of the play he continues fearful and uncertain. With joy he brings a ram, which he has
caught by the horn, to his father as the new
victim.

　　　" A scheppe, scheppe ! blyssyd mot thou be,
　　　　That ever thou were sent down heder,
　　　Thou schall thys day dey for me,
　　　In the worchup of the holy Tyynyte,
　　　　Now cum fast and goo we togeder
　　　　　To my fader of hevyn,
　　　Thow thou be never so jentyll and good,
　　　zyt had I lever thou schedyst thi blood,
　　　　I-wysse, scheppe, than I.
　　　Loo ! fader, I have browt here full smerte,
　　　　Thys jentyll scheppe,
　　　　And hym to you I zyffe.

But lord god, I thanke the with all my hart,
For I am glad that I schall leve,
And kys onys my dere moder."

But as the boy stoops to blow the fire for the sacrifice, he glances up at his father distrustfully.

Ysaac. And I wyll fast begynne to blowe,
Thys fyere schall brene a full good spyd ;
But, fader, wyll I stowppe downe lowe,
Ye wyll not kyll me with yowre sword, I trowe?

Abraham. Noo, harly,[1] swet son have no dred,
My mornyng is past.

Ysaac. A ! but I woold that sword wer in a glad,[2]
For i-wys, fader, yt make me full yll a gast.

Isaac is greatly relieved when the offering is over and they can leave the hill-top, which Abraham regards with a certain complacency.

Abraham. Loo ysaac, my son, how thynke ye
Be thys warke that we have wroght,
Full glad and blythe we may be
Ayens the wyll of god that we grucched nott,
Upon thys fayer hetth.

Ysaac. A ! fader, I thanke owr lord every dell,
That my wyt servyd me so wyll,
For to drede god more than my detth.

Abraham. Why dere-worthy son, wer thow a-dred?
Hardely, chyld, tell me thy lore.

Ysaac. Ya, be my feyth, fader, now hath I red,
I wos never soo afrayd before,

---

[1] heartily. [2] gleed = fire.

As I have byn at thyn hyll.
But be my feyth, fader, I swere
I wyll never more cume there,
But yt be ayens my wyll.

Abraham. Ya, cum with me, my owyn swet sonn,
And homward fast now let us goon.

Ysaac. Be my feyth, fader, thereto I grant,
I had never so good wyll to gon hom,
And to speke with my dere moder.

It is possible that we have another Norfolk play.
There is a Croxton play extant, but the county is
not designated, and there are towns by the name
of Croxton in at least five other English counties.
This drama is entitled *The Play of the Sacrament*,
and is not, strictly speaking, a Mystery at all. Nor
is it a Morality. It is believed to be the earliest
English drama extant, which has neither allegorical
characters, nor a plot founded on Biblical narrative,
or on the life of a saint. Yet it is essentially a
church play, dealing with the same general subject
that is blazoned upon the beautiful glass of the
Chapel of the Sacrament, in Brussels cathedral, —
the story of outrages offered by Jews to the sacred
Host, wherein our Lord was held to suffer a renewal
of His Passion.

It may possibly have been the case, but was far
more probably a matter of Christian slander, that
at various times during the thirteenth and four-

teenth centuries continental Jews obtained and transfixed in their synagogues consecrated wafers, whereupon it was devoutly maintained by the faithful, the Real Presence, thus crucified, was attested by miracle. In the continental accounts the offending Jews are invariably burned alive. Our English dramatist is more merciful. He is, in point of technique, rather a clever versifier, with a quick ear for alliteration, and his humour, though coarse, is abundant.

After a summary of the action delivered in alternating speeches by two vexillaries, who inform us, amongst other matter, that the scene is laid in Aragon, a Christian merchant, "Syr Arystory," takes the stage, boasting exultantly of his far-famed wealth. The Presbyter gives him a kindly reminder to thank for this great prosperity his God that died on rood. The merchant hurriedly assents, but is evidently too much preoccupied with worldly affairs to be deeply impressed by religious considerations. "Syr Arystory" withdrawing, the wily Jew Jonathas, attended by four other sons of Israel, Jason and Jasdon, Malcus and Masphat, succeeds him as speaker, apparently mounting a second scaffold, and proceeds in turn to make a dazzling report of his own treasures, needing no prompter to induce him to render praise therefor to "Almighty Machomet."

But amidst all his wealth of gems and fruits, the Jew has a trouble.

> " ye beleve of thes crysten men ys false as I wene
>   for ye beleve on a cake me thynk yt ys onkynd.
> And alle they seye how ye prest dothe yt bynd
> And be ye myght of hys word make yt flessh & blode
> And thus be a conceyte ye wolde make vs blynd
> And how yt shuld be he yt deyed upon ye rode."

His companions agree with him that this must be an idle tale, and propose that they put it to the proof, plotting to bribe "Syr Arystory" to steal the wafer from the altar for them. It is worthy of note that the motive assigned for this sacrilege is not one springing from hatred of Christ, but rather one born of honest perplexity and a desire to attain truth. The scene is shifted to the other platform. The Presbyter proposes to go to church to "say his evensong," and "Syr Arystory" promises him a good supper on his return. Meanwhile Peter Powle, "Syr Arystory's" clerk, presents the Jewish merchants to his master. Jonathas at once enters upon his business and makes a liberal offer, "clothe of gold, precyous stones & spyce plente," with twenty "pownd" thrown in, if the Christian will procure for him his "God in a cake." "Sir Arystory" is horrified at the impious suggestion, but when the bribe reaches a hundred pounds, thinks

better of it. At supper he plies the Presbyter
with wine, —

> " ther ys no precyouser fer nor nere
>   for alle wykkyd metys yt wylle dejest," —

and when the holy man has fallen into the pro-
found slumber consequent upon such deep potations,
"Syr Arystory" takes the church-keys, invades the
sacred choir, and delivers up the Host to Jonathas.
The Jew bears away his prize to the house where
the other Israelites await him, and here, after in-
creduously repeating one to another the Christian
history, they fall upon the wafer with their daggers,
pricking the five wounds in it, nailing it to a pillar,
and plucking it down again with pincers. It bleeds,
and the sight dismays and maddens them. Jonathas
attempts to throw the cake into a chaldron of boil-
ing oil, but it clings to his hand, and he runs up
and down like one in a frenzy. In the attempts
to detach the wafer, the hand of Jonathas is torn
off, and a quack doctor, who, with his boy Colle,
furnishes the comedy of the play, — and very low
comedy it is, — appears upon the scene. Meanwhile the wafer, hand and all, has been thrown into
the seething chaldron. The oil forthwith waxes
red as blood and overflows the vessel. In haste
Jason takes the pincers, plucks out the wafer, and
casts it into a red-hot oven. The oven bursts

asunder, the bleeding Image of Christ comes forth and pleads with His tormentors, who are heart-smitten, implore and receive pardon, even that blasphemous right hand of Jonathas being restored to him, make public confession and restitution, and undertake a penitential pilgrimage.

"The Story of the Creaĉon of Eve, with the Ex-pylling of Adam and Eve out of Paradyce," a grocers' pageant, was apparently one of a Norwich cycle of twelve Whitsun plays. This Mystery savours of Mo-rality, numbering among its characters Dolor and Mys-erye. It pays much heed, likewise, to musical effect. The opening scene exhibits the creation of Eve, a "Rybbe coloured Redde," which is counted among the stage properties of the guild, being taken by "Pater" out of "mañys syde" in the presence of the audience, and then and there transformed into a woman.

> " a ribbe out of mañys syde I do here take,
> bothe flesche & bone I do thys creatur blysse,
> And a woman I fourme, to be his make,
> Semblable to man ; beholde here she ys."

Adam expresses his thanks in English garnished with Latin, and is set by his Maker to keep the "Garden of Pleasure." On God's departure, Adam at once excuses himself to Eve.

> " O lovely spowse of God's creaĉon,
> I leve the here alone, I shall not tary longe,
> for I wylle walke a whyle, for my recreaĉon."

The Serpent, handsomely attired in a "cote with hosen, a tayle stayned," and a crown and wig, comes promptly upon the scene and induces Eve to taste the apple, claiming that he is sent by God to give her that command. Adam returns and partakes of the forbidden fruit. The voice of God is heard calling through the garden. Here occurs a hiatus in the manuscript, and the rest of the play, resuming with the driving of the guilty pair out of Paradise, is written in a more modern style. A second version of the story, as late as 1565, is added. Here, after the exile, Dolor and Myserye lay hold of Adam by both arms, and the Holy Ghost enters to comfort him with Gospel speech.

The subjects of the four plays which Mr. Furnivall has set the example of classing together as the Digby Mysteries, although only the first three are found in what is known as the Digby manuscript, are the "Killing of the Children or the Slaughter of the Innocents" (also entitled "Candlemas Day," or "Parfre's Candlemas Day," John Parfre being the name of the transcriber), the "Conversion of Saint Paul," "Mary Magdalene," and the "Burial and Resurrection of Christ,"—this last sometimes regarded as two plays instead of one. These Digby Mysteries, later than the York, the Towneley, the Coventry, the Chester, are by that so much the poorer, belonging to the decay of the old religious stage and pointing,

by their very restlessness and caprice, to the coming
change and the birth of the secular drama.

Candlemas Day apparently belonged to a New
Testament cycle of pageants, of which only one was
played each year.   In the prologue we read : —

> " The last year we shewid you in this place
>   how the shepherdes of Cristes birthe made letificacion,[1]
>   And thre kynges that come fro ther Cuntrees be grace
>   To worshipe Jesu, with enteer devocion."

And in the epilogue : —

> " Now of this pore processe we make an ende,
>   thankyng you all of your good attendaunce ;
>   and the next yeer, as we be purposid in our mynde,
>   The disputacion of the doctours to shew in your presens."

The play runs in the main on the old lines.   There
is the usual ranting Herod, by whose messenger,
Watkyn, the comic element is supplied.   Watkyn is
a Braggadocio, — a crude, dramatic anticipation of
Parolles and Bobadill.   Eager to be knighted, he
burns to distinguish himself in the Bethlehem affray,
but, as he involuntarily confesses, is grievously afraid
of the women.

> " I shall go shew your knyghtes how ye have seid,
>   And arme my-self manly, and go forth on the flokke ;
>   And if I fynde a yong child I shall choppe it on a blokke ;

---

[1] joy.

though the moder be angry, the child shalbe slayn,
but yitt I drede no thyng more than a woman with a Rokke,[1]
ffor if I se ony suche, be my feith I come a-geyn."

herowd.

what, shall a woman with a Rokke drive the a-way?
ffye on the traitour ! now I tremble for tene.
I have trosted the long and many a day ;
A bold man and an hardy I went thu haddist ben.

Watkyn, Messanger.

So am I, my lord, and that shalbe seen
that I am a bold man and best dare a-byde ;
And ther come an hundred women I wole not ffleen,
but fro morowe tyll nyght with them I dare chide ;
And therfor my lord ye may trust unto me,
for all the children of Israell your knyghtes and I shall kylle,
I wyll not spare on, but dede thei shalbe,
If the ffader and moder will lete me have my wille.

Herowd.

Thu hirdeyn, take hed what I sey the tyll,
And high the to my knyghtes as fast as thu can ;
say, I warne them in ony wyse þer blood þat thei spille
A-bought in every Cuntre, and lette for no man.

Watkyn.

Nay, nay, my lord, we wyll let for no man,
though ther come a Thousand on a rought ;[2]
for your knyghtes and I will kyll them all if we can,
but for the wyves, that is all my dought.

---

[1] distaff.   [2] rout.

And if I se ony walkyng a-bought,
I will take good hede till she be goon ;
And assone as I aspye that she is oute,
by my feith into the lions I will go Anon.
And thus I promyse you, that I shall never slepe,
but evermore wayte to fynde the children alone,
And if the moder come In under the benche I will crepe
And lye stille ther tyll she be goon ;
than manly I shall come out and hir children sloon,
And whan I have don, I shall renne fast a-way.
if she founde hir child dede, and toke me ther alone,
be my feith I am sure we shuld make a fray.

herowd.

Nay, harlott, a-byde stylle with my knyghtes, I warne the,
tyll the children be slayn all the hooll rought ;
and whan thu comyst home a-geyn I shall avaunce the
If thu quyte the like a man, whill thu art ought ;
And if thu pley the coward, I put the owt of dought,
of me thu shalt neyther have ffee nor advauntage ;
therfor I charge you the contre be well sought,
And whan thu comyst home, shalt have thi wage.

watkyn.

Yis, sire, be my trouthe ye shall wele knowe
whill I am oute how I shall aquyte me,
for I purpos to spare neither high nor lowe,
If ther be no man wole smyte me.
the most I fere the wyves will bete me ;
yitt shall I take good hert to me and loke wele a-bought,
And loke that your knyghtes be not ferre fro me,
For if I be alone I may sone gete a Clought.

The mothers are as good as his fears. They make a desperate resistance, and finally, when the children have been torn from their arms and butchered before their eyes, set upon Watkyn, and, with taunts of dubbing him knight with their distaffs, beat him until the bolder murderers are forced to come to his rescue.

This pageant has music and dancing after both prologue and epilogue. The second Digby Mystery, too, the Conversion of Saint Paul, was enlivened by dancing after the prologue and after the acts, for this play is remarkable as having been performed at three stations. In the first act, the fun is furnished by a scene of coarse comedy between the servant of Saul, the future apostle appearing as a knight-errant, and the ostler, who is inclined to put on airs. But the second act, which is taken up by Paul's conversion, and the third, which deals with his escape, through angelic agency, from the toils of Annas and Caiaphas, introducing, to boot, a sermon preached by him on the favourite text of the Seven Deadly Sins, were evidently considered dull, for a later hand has ingeniously inserted at the beginning of the third act, before the sermon, a carnival of consternation over the loss of Saul, among the devils in hell. If the stage directions were faithfully carried out, this episode doubtless redeemed the play from popular disfavour, for these directions promise flame and uproar in plenty. For instance, — "Here shall enter another devyll, callyd Mercurye, with a fyerying, comying in hast, cryeing and rorying." And ultimately the demons "vanyse away, with a fyre flame and a tempest."

Mary Magdalene is a play greatly confused in structure and of extraordinary length. It is divided by Dr. Furnivall into two parts, of which the first embraces twenty scenes and the second thirty-one. It required probably no less than four scaffolds for presentation, the Emperor Tiberius, Herod, Pilate, and the Devil each having his own platform. A ship was part of the stage furniture, and a castle, — the castle of Mary Magdalene besieged by the Devil and the Seven Deadly Sins. The three kings of the world, the flesh and the devil are in the cast, but their Majesties are quite overshadowed by the King of Marseilles, who performs the rôle of chief braggart. The plot is of the loosest. Tiberius, "of heven and hell chyff rewler," opens the play with brag and bluster and with threats against the Christians. Then is displayed the castle, whose lord, Cyrus, describes his three children, and makes in their presence his last will and testament.

> " Now Lazarus, my sonne, whech art þer brothyr,
> The lordshep of Jerusalem I gyff þe after my dysses,
> and mary, thys castell, a-lonly, an non othyr ;

& martha xall have beteny, I sey exprese :
thes gyftes I graunt you withowtyn les,
whyll þat I am in good mynd."

In the third scene Tiberius sends orders to Herod
to search out all rebels and heretics. In the fourth,
Herod, ranting in his accustomed fashion, learns
from his philosophers of the Messianic prophecies
and decides, his decision being sharpened by the
receipt of the Emperor's message, to seek for Christ
and put Him to death. Pilate then appears and
expresses himself to the same purport. The action
returns to the castle, where Cyrus, stricken with
mortal pains, blesses his children, dies, and leaves
them sorrowing. The seventh scene opens with
the ominous direction : "Her xal entyr þe kyng of
þe world, þen þe kyng of þe flesch, and þen þe dylfe,
with þe seven dedly synnes, a bad angyll an a good
angyl." The odds are evidently sorely against the
good angel. The king of the world expresses himself as the first of potentates, next to the King
of Heaven, telling how he guides the wheel of
fortune, and how in him rests the order of the
seven metals, knit each to a star, as gold to the
sun, silver to the moon, iron to Mars, quicksilver
to Mercury, red copper to Venus, brittle tin to
Jupiter, heavy lead to Saturn, — treasure with which
the seven princes of hell are enriched. Pride and
Covetousness applaud this address. The king of

the flesh then has his turn, declaring that he puts delight in flowers and spices, and in his spouse Luxuria, his knight Glutton, and his friend Sloth. Satan himself takes the word at last, and calls his peers and followers to hold consultation with him, as to how the fair castle of Mary Magdalene may be overthrown. The Seven Deadly Sins besiege the walls in vain and withdraw to Jerusalem, but Luxuria slips in, attended by the bad angel, flatters Mary, and persuades her to relieve her grief for her father's death by disporting herself abroad. They accordingly walk to Jerusalem and rest in a tavern, where a dandy, Curiosity, dances with Mary and leads her to fall in love with him. The bad angel speeds away to the devils with the news, and Luxuria is commanded by Satan to remain with the victim and keep her in sin. But while Mary, musing happily on her "valentynes, my byrd swetyngs, my lovys so dere," falls asleep in an arbour, Simon the Leper is planning a grand feast and wishing he could induce the new prophet, the report of whose "hye nobyll-nesse" is all abroad, to honour it by his presence. The good angel finds Mary, who, brought to repentance, resolves to seek help from Christ.

> " I xal porsue þe prophett, wherso he be,
>   for he is þe welle of perfyth charyte."

Then follows the beautiful scene at the feast, the seven devils, who are the Seven Deadly Sins, departing from Mary, as she sits forgiven at the Saviour's feet, while the bad angel, according to the stage direction, enters into hell, "with thondyr," and is there, with the seven devils, soundly chastised for his failure. Mary returns to Lazarus and Martha. The brother sickens, dies, is buried, and raised again, and with the joyous clamours of the multitude, turned by this miracle to faith in Jesus, the first part of the drama ends. Part II. is opened by the leading bully of the cast, the King of Marseilles, vaunting himself as the Head of Heathendom, and heaping praises on his queen, whom he styles the Beryl of Beauty. Then a devil, yelling frightfully, bursts in to tell how Christ has harried hell.

> "ower barres of Iron ar all to-brost! stronge gates of
> brasse!
> the king of Joy enteryd In þer-at, as bryth as fyr'ys
> blase!
> for fray of his ferfull baner, ower felashep fled
> asondyr;
> whan he towcheyd it, with his toukkyng þey brast
> as ony glase."

The three Marys next appear, lamenting the death of their Lord, but are comforted by the angels of the sepulchre. Mary Magdalene communes of these matters with Peter and John, and there follows the

dawn-scene in the garden.   Christ afterwards appears
to His mother and His disciples.   The action is then
transferred to the palace of the King of Marseilles,
who is preparing a great sacrifice to Mahound.   A
ribald dialogue ensues between the fat priest and
his profane boy.   This hopeful acolyte mocks the
priest's ministrations at the altar by gabbling after
him a nonsensical jargon, ending with a fervent wish
that the worshippers may all die on the gallows.
Next in order, Pilate sends word to Herod and
Tiberius that Jesus' disciples have robbed the sepulchre.   Christ appears in the heavens to Mary Magdalene, bidding her go to Marseilles and convert the
land.   "Here," says the stage direction, "xal entyre
a shyp with a mery song."   This is the barque that,
the shipman and his boy furnishing new buffoonery,
conveys Mary to Marseilles, where she receives but
an ill welcome from the king, until his idols quake
before her and his temple bursts into flame.   Then
he appears inclined to compromise, but breaks off
abruptly and goes to bed.   Angels bring Mary food,
and, walking before her in white mantles, bearing
tapers, lead her to the royal chamber.   The king
and queen, naturally impressed by the intrusion of
this procession, are converted, and give their goods
to feed the poor.   This done, in the same vessel that
brought Mary to Marseilles, the royal pair embark
on a voyage to the Holy Land, but on shipboard

the queen dies in childbirth. The dead mother and living infant are laid on a rock in the sea, and the king placidly continues his voyage. Having been baptised by Peter in Jerusalem, he returns in the same ship, and, chancing to pass the rock, is over-joyed to discover his baby plump and rosy, and — such was the grace of Mary Magdalene — the mother alive and well. The reunited family return to Marseilles, where they are greeted by Mary, who shortly after withdraws into the wilderness. Here she lives for thirty years as an anchorite, being thrice a day lifted up into the clouds and fed with manna. Save for one priest, she holds converse with none but angels. This priest administers to her the last sacrament and the heavens open to receive her, her celestial visitants welcoming their sister with "a mery song."

This long, illogical drama, in part Scriptural, in part legendary, and in part allegorical, is of interest as embracing the elements alike of Mystery, Saint Play, and Morality, but on literary grounds, at least, is certainly not without need of the apology which constitutes the epilogue : —

> "yff Ony thyng Amysse be,
> blame connyng, and nat me :
> I desyr þe redars to be my frynd,
> yff þer be ony amysse, þat to amend."

The use of the word "redars" here would seem to indicate that the Miracle Plays were beginning to gain a library footing.

The last Mystery of this group, the Burial of Christ and the Resurrection, in reality one play in two parts, has no touch of comedy. Diffuse and monotonous though the continual lamentations are, the drama is guiltless of offence against religious feeling. Some of the sequences of the Easter Mass were sung as part of the performance, which may well have taken place in the church, the first part on Good Friday and the second on Easter. The play is devoid of poetic merit, almost of dramatic character, and a few lines, for style and tone and tenor, may serve to sample the whole, as these from Joseph's lament : —

> " O calvery mount, on lengthe and brede !
> O calvery ! thy greyn colore is turnyd to rede
> By a blissed lammes bloode which now is dede."

In addition to this Miracle series already noted, Cornwall has a *Creation of the World*, which carries the Biblical story on through Noah's flood, and closes with an invitation to the audience to come early on the morrow to see the Passion Play. This *Creation* is of late date, though prior to 1611, and the un-known author imitates and often copies outright the *Origo Mundi*. His work, however, has certain indi-

vidual features. Lucifer argues his own case warmly
in opposition to God and the angels, Michael and
Gabriel being especially hot against the rebel. Cain,
whose character is much elaborated, not in amiable
directions, flees from home, after the murder, with
his wife Calmana by his side and their little children
upon his back, God having marked him by a horn in
the forehead. Lamech, as in the Coventry cycle,
slays his grandsire Cain by misadventure. Enoch
is translated, and Seth writes out the record of the
world in two books, for whose safe-keeping he erects
a pillar of brass and a pillar of marble. Tubal leads
the ridicule against Noah as he labours at the ark,
and Noah's wife has to be sharply summoned by her
husband before she enters, although she explains the
delay as due to her diligence in collecting the household goods.

> " Needful is it to save what there is.
>   I ought not to throw away.
>   Good it is for us to save them.
>   They cost a shower of money,
>   The same tackles that are here.
>   Fair Noah, thou knowest that."

Although English literature proper has, with
the doubtful exceptions of *Mary Magdalene* and
the Anglo-Saxon *Passion of Saint George*, no surviving Saint Plays, Cornwall cherishes a *Life of
Saint Meriasek*, a play founded on three legends

awkwardly fitted together,— the legend of Meriasek, son of a Duke of Brittany, who, for love of the priestly profession, refused marriage with a wealthy princess and led the life of a miracle-working hermit, first in Cornwall and afterwards in his native land ; the legend of Saint Sylvester, who healed the Emperor Constantine of leprosy by a dip in the baptismal font, and then aided him in establishing Christianity throughout his broad dominion ; and the curious legend of a mother who, on the Virgin's continued disregard of her prayer for the deliverance of a son in captivity, carried off the Christ-Child from the arms of the Virgin's statue, and refused to yield up the baby to the Madonna until her own son was restored to her.

This, so far as I am at present aware, closes our list of English Miracle Plays, although I would call attention to Ten Brink's account of a Miracle named by him *Jacob and Esau*, not to be confounded with the Elizabethan *Jacob and Esau* printed in Hazlitt's Dodsley. There are, it is true, various other productions often referred to as Mysteries, but not, it would seem to me, in a strict use of the term. Of these the *Harrowing of Hell*, a dramatic poem rather than a drama, has received much notice from scholars because of its undoubted antiquity. The Protestant Mysteries of Bishop Bale — Bilious Bale, as his enemies nicknamed him — are curiosities in

English literature. The polemical Bishop laid vio-
lent hold of this old-fashioned dramatic instrument,
forged in the mediæval church, and attempted to
wield it in behalf of the Reformed Faith. He wrote
a series of what he was pleased to style comedies,
intending that these should form a continuous history of the life of Christ. The plays are lost, but
something of their character may be gathered from
their titles, the author's own list being extant : —

1. *Of Christ, when He was twelve years old*, one
   comedy.
2-3. *Of His Baptism and Temptation*, two comedies.
4. *Of Lazarus raised from the Dead*, one comedy.
5. *Of the Councills of the Bishops*, one comedy.
6. *Of Simon, the Leper*, one comedy.
7. *Of the Lord's Supper and washing the feet*, one
   comedy.
8-9. *Of the Passion of Christ*, two comedies.
10-11. *Of the Sepulture and Resurrection*, two comedies.

But Bale wrote other plays, both religious and
political. Of the latter, a blending of the historical
drama with the Morality, but one specimen, *Kyng
Johan*, remains. Of Bale's distinctively religious
plays, four are extant. One of these, *The Three
Laws of Nature, Moses, and Christ*, is still in manuscript, but the others have made their way into
print. *God's Promises* is modelled after the *Pro
cessus Prophetarum* of the genuine Miracle Cycle,

but, as Pollard says, " has a tediousness all its own."
The interpretation of the divine nature is, however,
the most offensive feature in the play. *Pater
Cœlestis* displays himself in debate harsh, blunt, and
acrimonious beyond all heresy. No wonder that
Noah says : —

> " Blessed be thy name, most Mighty Merciful Maker,
> With Thee to dispute it were inconvenient."

Or that Abraham asks : —

> " Tell me, blessed Lord, where will thy great malice light?
> My hope is, all flesh shall not perish in thy sight."

But the attitude of this bitter deity toward man is
best summed up in the sententious line : —

> " In my syghte he is more venym than the spyder."

One is tempted to remind the Bishop that God
created the spider, too. *John the Baptyste's preachynge in the Wyldernesse*, partisan and unpoetic though
it is, broadens to a more genial handling of its
theme, and as regards the last of these controversial
dramas, *The Temptation of Christ*, it may at least
be said, though it is not much to say, that the
bearing and address of Jesus toward the tempter
compare favourably, for dignity, courtesy, and for-
bearance, with those of Milton's Christ in the *Paradise Regained.*

What would have been the result, one wonders, if Milton had carried out his design of casting the theme of *Paradise Lost* upon the lines of a Miracle Play? At all events, it would have been more successful than Byron's Mysteries, — even than Byron's *Cain*.

CHAPTER IV.

MIRACLE PLAYS — DRAMATIC VALUES.

THERE are two ways of regarding our old Miracle
Plays. Many students of English literature think of
them confusedly, contemptuously, as the primal dramatic chaos out of which the Elizabethan stage rose,
not by process of evolution, but by divine fiat, —
"Let there be Shakespeare," and there was Shakespeare. Others see in this five-centuried growth not
merely the dramatic elements, but those displayed on
a grand scale and already shapen into a huge, rough-
hewn, majestic Gothic drama. They see in the
Miracle Play not merely collision, but tremendous
clash of conflict; not merely scheme, but inevitable
development of event from event, and these events
colossal; not merely life-like characterisation, but
realised humanity, deviltry, and Divinity; not merely
passion, but all the passion that surged through the
great, child-like, mediæval heart. The upholders of
this second view must to a large degree ignore
detail, often uncouth, often unseemly, often ridicu-

lous, and persistently fix attention upon the mass
of the Miracle structure, the sweep of outline, and
dignity of design. They must have limitless forbear-
ance for the halting, tedious, undeveloped speech, —
that most beggarly attire with which the vast idea is
clothed upon. No poet ear listened for the cadences
that should form a fitting music for the splendid
spectacle. No poet brain brooded the mighty
thought until mighty language was born to compass it. Feeble linguists, uncertain melodists, dull
versifiers, toiled over those tattered play-books, whose
inherent drama was no one man's invention, no one
nation's achievement, but the life-pulse of mediæval
Christendom.

The composite authorship of the cycles is, indeed,
a critical problem of delightful difficulty, which has
already claimed much attention from scholars, Ten
Brink's analysis being the most thorough up to date,
and will undoubtedly claim more. The relation of
group to group, with all the concomitant study of
interpolations, adaptations, and possible foreign origi-
nals, is a subject that will not fail of patient and per-
severing investigation. Meanwhile it is, we trust,
permissible to note with the naked eye, over the
click of all these crowding German microscopes, the
general aspects of the dramatic conglomerate.

What is the stuff of these old Miracle Plays?
From what quarries was their varied material taken?

These bright-hued pageants, where the silent story of rich-stained glass and fresco came to life in breathing, moving figures, have indeed been designated a living *Biblia Pauperum*, but many of the *dramatis personæ* are unknown to Hebrew annalist or evangelist. It is in the Cornwall Plays, however, that we meet with the largest admixture of legend, and the statement may be admitted that the Keltic peoples, as a rule, gave in their Mysteries more place to fable, while the Teutonic held more closely to the Biblical text. Our English Miracles sprang from a Saxon-Norman stock, in some cases, notably in that of the Coventry Plays, under strong French influence, and so present a blending of record and of legend, the record predominating. Without going into the minutiæ of the subject, the chief sources of Miracle material in England may be ranked as the Vulgate, the Apocryphal Gospels, and the manners of the time, especially among the poorer classes.

The handling of Old Testament subjects was, as has been seen, marked by extraordinary freedom. To the vision of the Creation, received as literal history, was persistently added the wild, feudal legend of the Fall of Lucifer, — a legend which twice in English literature has attained epic grandeur: once with the inspired dreamer, Cædmon, and once with the Puritan protagonist, Milton. The story of Cain and Abel was embellished by the transforma-

tion of Cain into a Northumbrian boor. The story
of the Ark was saturated with fun arising from the
vixenish characteristics which, in an astonishing
outburst of posthumous slander, the Miracle dramatists have well-nigh universally agreed in bestowing
upon Noah's wife. Upon the story of Abraham and
Isaac was lavished all the wealth of tenderness and
pathos and homely piety which lie deep at the roots
of English domestic life. These are the main
themes taken from the Old Testament by the
Miracle writers, and the additions are, on the whole,
less of the nature of legend than of bold and spirited
elaboration, — an elaboration carried out on purely
mediæval and English lines, without the faintest
attempt at reproducing either the life of the patriarchal ages or the customs of the East.

When we come to the New Testament history,
we recognise at once the false strands in the web, —
the incidents and characterisations drawn from the
Apocryphal Gospels. These gospels had their *raison
d'être* in a natural curiosity to know more of the
personal life of Jesus Christ than is recorded in the
canonical books. Such fragments of tradition as
were abroad relating to Joseph and Mary and their
kindred, to the birth and childhood of the Redeemer,
to His trial and crucifixion, the fate of His perse-
cutors, the future of His friends, found their way
into written narrative, sometimes introductory, some-

times appendical, but always supplementary to the Evangelical accounts. The works of the early Christian Fathers, Justin, Irenæus, Clement of Alexandria, and others, contain a few passages apparently confirmatory of some of these traditions, as in the query of Athanasius, occurring in his treatise on the "Incarnation of the Word," — a query which would demonstrate the Godhood of Christ by the method of comparison : "Who, among righteous men or kings, went down into Egypt and the idols of Egypt fell ?" With such evidence in their favour, it is in no way remarkable that the mother-church attached great importance to the Apocryphal Gospels, incorporating certain stories from them into the Roman breviary and service-books. That famous compilation of mediæval myths, the *Legenda Aurea*, drew largely from these spurious narrations. The Apocryphal Gospels were, indeed, extremely popular throughout the Middle Ages, being read, translated, paraphrased, and reproduced in many literary forms, as well as in painting, and, above all, in the sculpture, wood-carving, and glass-staining of the cathedrals. But, confining attention to the field of literature, it is said that versions of these Apocryphal stories have been discovered not only in Britain, France, Spain, Germany, Italy, but in Greece, Egypt, Syria, Persia, India, and as far north as Iceland. In English literature, they found expression not only in the religious drama, but in homilies, histories, and carols.

The longer one dwells on the Apocryphal Gospels, the more one comes to appreciate the omissions of the Mystery writers, — their comparative reticence in regard to the many legends of Christ's infancy and boyhood, and in regard to much else that closely concerned His person. In general, the old playwrights contented themselves with borrowing from the spurious accounts more or less matter relating to the marriage of Joseph and Mary, and to Joseph of Arimathea, the Harrowing of Hell, the fate of Pilate, with his vain efforts to shelter himself within the seamless vesture, the ascension and coronation of the Virgin, and the legends of Veronica, who was believed to have stood among the weeping women by the Via Dolorosa, and have received upon her handkerchief, still exhibited as a holy relic at Rome, the impress of the Saviour's face, — a woman identified in the Apocrypha with her who had an issue of blood twelve years and was healed by Jesus. The Gospels of Nicodemus, which are of the nature of appendices to the canonical books, are the most celebrated of the New Testament Apocrypha. From these Gospels of Nicodemus is taken, amongst much other matter, the *Harrowing of Hell*, with many of its familiar accessories, such as the meeting of the rescued souls, on their entrance into Paradise, with

Enoch and Elijah, soon joined by the thief from
Calvary, bearing his cross upon his shoulder.

Tribute should be paid to the taste of the early
English dramatists in so largely ignoring another
class of legends besides those relating to the personal life of Jesus. It has been noted already that
the list of English religious dramas, apart from the
Latin compositions of Hilarius, comprises little in
the way of Saint Plays. Probably some such plays
have been lost. Protestantism, which barely toler-
ated the Mysteries, would hardly have suffered anything so unmistakably Romish as a Saint Play to
show itself by daylight. Yet much which was more
alien than these to the spirit of the Reformation
lived on in the dark, and if there had ever existed
any considerable number of Saint Plays, assuredly
records and allusions relating to them, if not the
very manuscripts, would have been preserved. When,
therefore, one remembers the multitude of such
miraculous legends afloat through the Middle Ages,
how they invaded almost every department of literature, — chronicles, homilies, even Chaucer's *Canterbury Tales*, — the Mystery writers are again to be
commended for what they have left unsaid.

After all, in the depths of the English heart there
is, and ever has been, a sense of the Divine, — the
saving salt of any literature and of any nation. It
was this sense which, working obscurely and often

dubiously, guided these rude old playwrights in their selection of dramatic subjects and in their handling of the subjects chosen. Badly as they bungled the Christian story, the person of Christ was always sacred to them. With the minor characters, as Joseph and the Christmas shepherds, they did not hesitate to take enormous liberties; but no touch of burlesque mars the majesty of that central figure. It is true that the speeches assigned to Christ are sometimes stiff and dull, — at their best, a weak dilution of the Gospel text; but this was due to inadequacy of literary art, not to irreverence of spirit.

As sources of the Miracle Plays, it should be added, the Vulgate and the New Testament Apocrypha served as remote springs, original fountainheads, rather than the immediate feeding streams. The incidents of the Apocryphal Gospels, in particular, were commonly taken not from the text itself, but from the legends of the text as caught up into current speech and art and story.

The Miracle Cycle, then, has for its fundamental material the Christian faith, crudely comprehended, given with startling realism personal embodiment and physical environment, sprinkled over with legend and anachronistic touches of rural English life, yet still in essential features the Christian history.

There is intrinsic dramatic quality in the theme, however conceived. No greater theme is possible to art than this. But as conceived by the Middle Ages, the Christian story is frankly and forcibly dramatic. For the power of these cycles lies in their mighty range. It is the complete history of God's creation that they depict, — a history dramatically treated. The Mystery playwright knew no philosophy of evil as the mere negation of good. To his vision the earth was the arena where two tremendous Spirits, the Eternal God and the Archfiend of Rebellion, wrestled in strong contention over the soul of man. We see these two towering figures in their first encounter; we witness Satan's overthrow, followed so soon by his fateful triumph in the garden; we pursue the bitter consequences of that triumph through scenes of strife and disaster, — the murderous blow of Cain and Lamech's fatal archery, God's hand appearing here and there to snatch His righteous servant from the flood, or His chosen people from the bondage of Egypt. Then are heard the chanting voices of the procession of prophets, foretelling the advent of a glorious champion for humanity, even the Son of God. Hereat the Powers of Evil wax more furious and malignant. Herod rages, the Pharisees plot, Judas betrays, the soldiers seize, the disciples fall away, the judges exult, the tormentors scourge and mock, the mob denies, Pilate condemns, the cross uplifts its burden, and the victory of Satan would seem to be complete. But the heart of the spectator is enwrapt by a strange hope and confidence. From the first silver shining of the Bethlehem star upon that peaceful group, the fair young mother with the child clasped to her breast, shepherds kneeling at her feet, and kings hastening to offer gifts, all through that life of ineffable sacrifice and suffering, grace and majesty, to the darkening of the heavens above Mount Calvary, from whose central cross gleams the motionless white figure, there has been ripening in men's minds an apprehension of a new force born into the world, the all-conquering force of love, before which even the bolts and bars of hell shall yet give way. Thus in crudely dramatic fashion that wan and tortured form rises from the sepulchre in kingly might, descends the black and sheer approach to Satan's fortress, bursts the gates of brass, is locked in terrible wrestle with the arch-enemy soon overthrown, and leads out of those deep dungeons up to the light of Paradise the victims of the gay deceiver's craft. Then are beheld the ascension of Christ the Son and Mary Mother, the gratulation of the angel hosts, a last struggle of Satan in the shape of Antichrist, renewed victory of the Son of Man, and the final awful spectacle of Doom, with the bliss of Paradise on

Christ's right hand and the torments of Purgatory on his left.

So for a long summer's day, or for three days, or for nine, scene after scene the great tragedy flashed by, and the eyes of the attendant multitude read it literally as the creed of their own belief, the book of their own life, and their hearts swelled or fainted, melted or were enraptured within them.

It was all so very real in those centuries of faith and art and passion. The French Miracle scaffold, with the heaven-stage above and the hell-stage below, both intent on the earth-stage between, graphically confesses the mediæval conception of the universe. No Copernicus had yet arisen to daunt men's minds by the disclosure that this marvellous world of theirs was but one of an innumerable host of stars, weaving "the web of the mystic measure" through the wilderness of space. The personal being and eventful history of Lucifer were not in question. That smoke-blackened monster, with crooked horns and snout, peering with menacing aspect out of hellmouth, wore the veritable likeness of the fallen archangel, ever on the scent for prey. There was no old school and no new school of Old Testament criticism, with wordy debate of myth and scribe and epoch. Noah's Ark was as genuine a craft to the fourteenth century as the *Pinta* is to us, and Eve's apple far more certain

than Wilhelm Tell's. Most significant of all, no
Strauss, no Renan, even no Channing, had troubled
the ear of those primitive play-goers. It was the
semblance of their very God they saw in the child
clinging to Mary's neck, in the boy questioning the
white-bearded Rabbis, in the youth baptised by
John in Jordan, in the patient sufferer wounded
for their transgressions and bruised for their in-
iquities. With what white lips the men looked
upon, how the women turned their faces from the
crucifixion! It was no mere spectacle. It was no
mere historic execution. It was truth itself, — the
truth by which they lived. And Doomsday! In
the other pageants it was the past revived in change-
ful picture, but this is future for each appalled beholder. Have not the clergy taught how the mighty
contest between God and Satan is waged not only
for humanity in mass, but for every human soul?
The Devil has lost the larger stake. Hell has been
emptied once, but there is Purgatory still, and there
is the consciousness of unshriven sin and the dread
of the demons' grip.

Allowing for all crudities of comprehension, still
the conception is colossal. So long as light strives
against darkness and good against evil, so long will
the theme retain its power. And not only this, but
so long as spirit is housed in flesh and fact made
manifest through form, the theme will lend itself to

art and compel that art either to some vague correspondence, as in Cimabue's Virgin,

> "planned
> Sublimely in the thought's simplicity,"

or to clear correspondence, as in the masterpieces of Raphael, with its own magnitude. The soulless must make men and women soulless, the abstract must make men and women abstract, before these can eradicate from humanity the spiritual craving for spiritual life, or the concrete need of concrete revelation of that life.

> " For Wisdom dealt with mortal powers,
> Where truth in closest words shall fail,
> When truth embodied in a tale
> Shall enter in at lowly doors."

What license of poetic imagery we allow to Milton, we may better allow to the Miracle playwrights. For Milton is hardly sincere with his Ptolemaic universe, his crystal, "orbs involving and involved," his classic hell, circumscribed by the river of oblivion, his seraphic gunners waving their fire-tipt reeds above the triple row of cannon. But our mediæval dramatists are supremely sincere. If they used imagery, they did not know it. If they personified, they did not mean it. If the truth was not the symbol, and the symbol not the truth, they did not distinguish. Nevertheless, they had the theme, and the theme shaped their dramatic art, as it shaped their plastic art, rudely indeed, but greatly. That most appreciative of the Miracle critics, the late Mr. Symonds, has recognised this power in several of the sub-themes handled in the cycles :—

" Language in the Miracles barely clothes the ideas which were meant to be conveyed by figured forms ; meagrely supplies the motives necessary for the proper presentation of an action. Clumsy phrases, quaint literalism, tedious homilies clog the dramatic evolution. As in the case of mediæval sculpture, so here the most spontaneous and natural effects are grotesque. In the treatment of sublime and solemn themes we may also trace a certain ponderous force, a dignity analogous to that of fresco and mosaic. Subjects which in themselves are vast, imaginative, and capable of only a suggestive handling, such as the Parliaments of Heaven and Hell, Creation, Judgment, and the Resurrection from the dead, when conceived with positive belief and represented with the crudest realism, acquire a simple grandeur."

It is that very effect of "simple grandeur" which I would claim for the Miracle Cycles as a whole, viewed from a sufficient distance, where details are lost in the general outline and relief. The cycle is the drama, of which the pageants are but shifting scenes. A grand dramatic framework is discernible through the awkward language and the naïve ideas. In all the groups, York, Towneley, Chester, Coventry, the cyclic features are the same. Lucifer puts himself in defiant antagonism to God, Who smites him and his adherents down to hell, creating Adam and Eve that they and their descendants may fill the vacant seats of heaven. The motives for the fierce Satanic warfare against God and man are thus made plain, — revenge and jealousy. Strife is henceforth an assured element. We have the dramatic opposition and the dramatic anticipation of a clash. Although the Titan combatants do not meet face to face, we see evil warring against good in the Cain pageant, the Pharaoh pageant, the Balaam pageant, while the chorus of the prophets leads expectation forward to the second act. Here God, in the person of Christ, openly takes the field against Satan, but in the Coventry cycle alone is the Devil brought much upon the stage to oppose Him. The temptation in the wilderness, which Milton sets, as crucial point, against the fall of man, the old dramatists pass hastily over, reserving their climax for the Harrowing of Hell. They like to represent the wily adversary as prescient of this storming of his feudal hold and as striving by the instrumentality of Pilate's wife to avert the crucifixion. None the less is Calvary the apparent victory of Satan. The two great battle-chiefs have closed at last, and God is overthrown. But there is a third act to come, the triumph-act of Christ, opening with the Harrowing of Hell and closing with the Judgment.

Even such, in outline, is the structure of that Elizabethan drama which the ruder Miracle drama fathered. Still the theme is rebellion against the divine law, as Macbeth rebelled, as Antony rebelled, as Faustus rebelled, each to be dashed to death against the right he had defied. Still, although technically the first and last acts are each sub-divided into two, the action progresses through three main movements, from cause to climax, from climax to consequence. Still there is the subtle effect of gain through loss, fainter lights cast from Calvary being shed on such sights as "the tragic loading" of that couch where the Desdemona-heart of love, the Othello-heart of faith have triumphed even in defeat over the Iago-heart of malice. Still there is the mighty range of the old drama, "rough, unswayable, and free." Elizabethan tragedy, with the careless strength of a young giant, shook off the troublesome conventions of the stage, unity of time, unity of place. Was not England reared upon dramas that embraced heaven, earth, and hell within their limits, that encompassed all of time that had been and yet should be? What did it matter, after that, if Perdita and Marina grew from babyhood to womanhood in a single afternoon, or the scene in the Globe playhouse was shifted back and forth between pre-Christian Britain and Renascence Italy? May not Shakespeare be forgiven even for providing

Bohemia with that unhappy sea-coast and letting Julio Romano be contemporary with the Delphic oracle, when we remember how his antecedent playwrights made Noah swear by St. John, and Pharaoh by Mahound, the shepherds of Bethlehem drink Ely ale, and Joseph and Mary be arraigned before the Bishop and his ecclesiastical court? Shall heedlessness of detail call out a sharper criticism than falseness or feebleness of conception? The Gothic drama abounded in robust vitality. Its nerves were not worn by overmuch civilisation. It was not easily shocked. A strain of heathen ferocity showed in it even to the end, — to Hamlet, to the Duchess of Malfi. Greek authority might enjoin the relation, rather than the portrayal, of deeds of bloodshed, violence, and horror, but Kyd and Webster were scions of a race that had looked for generations upon the Bethlehem massacre, the Harrowing of Hell, Calvary, and Doomsday.

But if the Miracle Cycle is to be held responsible for the Elizabethan disregard of the more artificial dramatic canons, the Elizabethan carelessness in minutiæ, and even the lingering brutalities of the Elizabethan stage, it must not be forgotten that these same rude Mysteries set examples not only of sweeping scope and massive structure, but of truth to human life. Unity of action is as binding on the old York playwright as on Shakespeare him-

self.   But this sovereign law of the drama was
observed by the mediæval playwrights, as by the
Elizabethan, less because they consciously proposed
to observe it than because it was inherent in the
material they had chosen.   Their plots were woven
not in fallible human brains, but in the loom of
Life, unerring artist.   Here and there an Elizabethan strove to be original.   Tourneur spun his
own plots and spoiled his tragedies.   But Shakespeare was content to take a tragedy that had been
lived and make it live again.   These stories on
which he flashed the prismatic light of his genius
had their strands already deep dyed with actual
blood and tears.   He could not greatly offend
against the prime dramatic law, while he walked
with Plutarch and with Holinshed, who had walked
with men.   In like manner the Miracle playwrights
have the Biblical record chiefly to thank for the
unity of action that marks the Miracle Cycle.

Yet granting this, the selective quality, which is
the dramatist's distinctive gift, has an indispensable
part to play.   Any student of Shakespeare who
has compared *Lear, King John, Henry the Fifth,*
with the so-called "old plays," though but a few
years earlier, on the same themes, needs no more
impressive revelation of the function of the artist.
As the architect compels the weight of stone and
marble to the soaring arch and airy tower that in

perfected beauty haunt his vision, so the dramatist selects and disposes his no less stubborn material in strict conformity with that one controlling action, that one organic human deed, — seed and flower and fruit, — which he recognises and reveals by prerogative of genius.

The Mystery playwrights possessed in rudimentary form this dramatic sense. The Miracle Cycle had grown up about the three liturgical dramas of Christmas, Good Friday, and Easter, and to these it shaped itself throughout, concentrating attention on Christ the champion, and keeping steadily in view the great collision toward which the forces of good and evil were converging. Guided by this principle of unity, the early dramatists resolutely denied themselves many an effective pageant from the Old Testament. The story of Abraham and Isaac, it is true, appealed to their sense of pathos too strongly to be excluded, but even Balaam and Pharaoh, pageants not altogether out of connection with the trend of the divine event, were individual experiments that did not win the general consent of the cyclists. The Cornwall dramatist, freer of fancy than his Saxon neighbours, ventured on the story of David, but found himself forced to bind it to the rest by the legend of the three miraculous rods. Likewise in dealing with the Gospel narrative, there is a tendency to subordinate not only the temptation scene, which might anticipate the triumph of Christ over Satan, reserved for the Harrowing of Hell, but also the Lazarus scene, lest this should forestall the continued victory of Christ in His breaking the bonds of death, reserved for the Resurrection pageant.

In addition to the sense of dramatic unity, these simple playwrights clearly had the sense of dramatic situation. This we continually encounter from the initial *Creatio*, where Satan, usurping his Maker's throne and receiving the homage of one-tenth the host of heaven, is cut short in his blasphemous boasts by the approach of God, and by the mere aspect of that dread figure is smitten down to hell, to the final *Damnatio*, where each song of thanksgiving from the throng of the saved is answered by a wail of agony from the throng of the lost, the white Christ standing calm above the tumult, with blessing in His outstretched right hand and cursing in His left.

One important feature of the Miracle Cycle, a feature which the Elizabethan drama duly inherited and fearlessly appropriated, remains to be noted, — the blending of comedy with tragedy. It can easily be conceived that to the devout spectator the heart-strain of the Passion pageants was almost intolerable. Very clear, it is true, was the shining background of divine love, with its promise of divine victory. As any master tragedy, from Æschylus to Browning, gives strange delight, in place of overwhelming pain, because the dark shadow-tracery throws into brighter relief the firm beauty of righteousness behind, so the assured faith of the mediæval audience made Whitsuntide and Corpus Christi, with their solemn spectacles, soul-refreshing holidays. The Christian tragedy met the basal requirement of Aristotle in that the minds of the beholders were purified by pity and by terror. But still the foreground effect was one of suffering, and the responsive sympathy was exhaustingly intense. In the drama, as in life, there was need of comedy to relieve the tension of emotion. The early playwrights, as the early carvers, were pupils of nature, and did not dream that anything which pertained to life could be alien to art. The grotesque seems to have been spontaneous with both classes of workmen, and, to a degree, unconscious. Reference here is had rather to the significantly intrusive figures and the studied comic rôles. It is life that gives warrant for the imp in the angel choir of Lincoln. It is life that gives warrant for Noah's thorny-tempered wife and sheepish old Joseph. And art, in holding close to life, finds herself the gainer. As the humours of the grave-digger throw into deeper shadow the waiting churchyard, with its open grave, and Hamlet's brooding heart, as King Lear's elemental agony of wrath shows more pitiful beside the whim-

sies of his sweet and bitter fool, so have the Miracle
Cycles artistic need of their scolding dame and
blundering old carpenter.

Shakespeare gave his august sanction to this fidelity of the Gothic drama to life. The musicians pass
their idle jests while, to all appearance and belief,
death lies on Juliet

> " like an untimely frost
> Upon the sweetest flower of all the field."

The black passion of Shylock is encircled by mirthful romance. And more and more, with Shakespeare's ever deepening comprehension of humanity,
the comedy presses nearer and nearer to the very
seat of tragedy. The helplessness of king and husband before the unbridled tongue of Paulina pro-
vokes the smile of the bystanding lords, even in
their painful apprehension for Hermione. Out of
his cloud of gloom Hamlet will still make sombre
sport of "tedious old fools," and Timon's angry
eyes must bear to be confronted by a burlesque
of his own life-wasting misery in Apemantus.

The earliest of the great English realists, Chaucer,
a secular dramatist born before the secular drama,
holds the mirror up to life as frankly as does
Shakespeare. But the star-bright idealists, Marlowe, Spenser, Shelley, are hopelessly at a loss
before the comic. Lovers of Marlowe trust that

most of his comic scenes, gross and pointless as they too often are, were written for him. The audience knew, and Marlowe knew, that comedy, though not such comedy, should relieve the terror of *Faustus*, but it was not in him to find and furnish it, for the idealist is a runaway from the school of life to the far-horizoned uplands of dreamland. Such truants are enviable in their escape from the coarse and the degrading. It is with the realistic comedy of Chaucer and Shakespeare that there come in the vulgar jokes and all that offensive indecency of expression which Chaucer so cheerily and ingeniously maintains is required by the laws of realistic art.

Turning from the structural principles of the Miracle Cycle to its characterisation, we meet again the realistic method. The third main source of Miracle material is to be looked for in the rural life of mediæval England, especially among the shepherds of Yorkshire and Lancashire, merry of mood, even in their poverty, and especially by the humble domestic hearth, where, no less than in Wordsworth's day, the baby boy lay busied with his mimic games,

> " Fretted by sallies of his mother's kisses,
>   With light upon him from his father's eyes."

There is no one feature of these rude old dramas more winning than the warmth of sympathy they evince with all the pure and tender, wholesome and generous brood of household affections. It was this kindly touch of nature which so endeared the Abraham pageant to these simple audiences, which stirred them to such vehement wrath against Herod, murderer of the innocents, which gave its beauty to the group about the manger, its pathos to the group about the cross, which made the women wail and sway in unison with the long lament of the Mater Dolorosa, as the lacerated body of her son was laid across her knees.

It is palpably absurd that these oriental scenes, dating from the dawn of the Christian era or from dim patriarchal times, should be given a fourteenth-century Northumbrian or Midland setting. The immediate cause was ignorance. The insular monks and tradesmen who composed and presented these plays were without information as to the customs of the East and of antiquity. Possibly there was also a remote cause. If the populace of Rome so late as the seventeenth century implicitly believed that the Divine Tragedy had been enacted within their own city at the very spots where they were accustomed to see it represented by the erection of a manger, or a cross, the scattering of palms, or the strewing of cypress boughs, it is not strange that mediæval simplicity made the Christian story so inherent a part of English life as to feel no incongruity in framing the Holy Family in a Yorkshire environment. At the heart of this folly lay, perhaps, a sleeping wisdom, in that the drama of Palestine is indeed not bound to locality or date, but belongs to all peoples and to all time.

The characterisation in the Mysteries is purely realistic, with the vividness of actual portraiture, where it concerns the rank and file of society. Noah's wife — for the Noah of the Mysteries is a yeoman — might have joined, with her distaff, any gossiping group of "spinsters in the sun" from Lancashire to Devon, and held her own in racy monologue against the Wife of Bath herself. The Coventry sompnour would have out-roared in jovial fellowship his boisterous brother of the "fyr-reed cherubynnes face," and one can readily picture the Bethlehem shepherds, chafed as they were by their social discontents, listening on the village green with confirmatory nods and frowns, while some gaunt clerk of Oxenford read aloud from well-thumbed manuscript a canto of *Piers Plowman.* Democratic satire of a burly, good-natured sort painted the ranting tyrants, Pharaoh and Cæsar, Herod and Pilate, but whatever secular criticism might have manifested itself in the delineation of the ecclesiastics was kept down by the clerical authorship or revision.

The Mystery treatment of the devils is amusing in its childish egotism. They are viewed simply as the enemies of the human race. After the first plunge of Lucifer and his faction into hellmouth, their deviltry is taken for granted, and their doom accepted as irreversibly sealed. Their rôle in the universe is settled, their costume determined, and nobody wonders about the look behind the mask. Later centuries may wax inquisitive. Milton may trace the deterioration of Lucifer, the fading of the bright archangelhood. Mrs. Browning may seek to comprehend the fire of his torment : —

> " that fire-hate
> *　　*　　*　　*　　*
> Wherein I, angel, in antagonism
> To God and His reflex beatitudes,
> Moan ever in the central universe
> With the great woe of striving against Love."

But our Mystery poets are supremely unconcerned as to the secrets of demon consciousness. Their presentation is distinctly objective. The devils are shown at their work, and busy enough about their mischievous labours, and pleased enough with their numerous successes these agents of evil seem to be. In their loss of spiritual susceptibility, they appear rather of the Mephistophiles type, but among their victims is no Faustus to wreak his restless curiosity upon them and force their frightful confidence. The human personages of the Miracle Cycles evidently regard the devils much as pioneers regard wild beasts, scientific inquiry being suspended for terror of claws and teeth. The very simplicity of the characterisation makes these grotesque fiends graphic and, in crude fashion, dramatically effective. Yet, although they sometimes gave an impressible man the nightmare, the average spectator had a lurking affection for the lesser devils. They were all he had left of the goblins, kobolds, and pixies of his ancestral heathenism. As for Satan himself, there was a delicious excitement in viewing the shaggy monster on the pageant scaffold, with God or Christ at hand to hurl him down presently into hellmouth. Seeing Satan off the stage might be quite another matter.

The characterisation of the third class of *dramatis personæ*, divine and angelic beings, was attended by graver dangers, which the Miracle Cycles did not escape. The first authority in English drama, Mr. Ward, says in regard to this:—

" These Mysteries teach, in their way, the lesson which the strange oaths of the Middle Ages teach in another, that a constant familiarity with the bodily presentment of sacred persons and things bred a material grossness in the whole æsthetical atmosphere of the people."

This is a serious charge, and one which cannot be gainsaid. As the gilt peruke grew familiar, the dream of the halo faded away. As the attire and demeanour of the celestial beings became conventionalised and hackneyed, the commonplaces of the pageant scaffold, the uplift and the glory of conception melted and were gone. The stage properties hung like clogs on the wings of heavenly imagination.

But if this be true of the æsthetic influence of the Miracles, what must have been their religious effect? That they were originally charged with devout passion who can doubt? Christendom was more than any nation. The Church enfolded all. Within the vast embrace of her beautiful walls there was room for all of human life, its mirth and sin and sorrow, its household charities and altar mysteries, its broken human loves and baffled Godward longings. Perhaps no one of the essential dramatic elements is stronger in the Miracles than the element of passion. Playwrights, actors, audience, all combined in flooding these unkempt plays with irresistible fervours and ardours. These were religious, but not as later centuries understand the term. Not exclusive, but inclusive, was that consecrated passion which carved waggish designs on the misereres of Chester cathedral, and called forth peal on peal of laughter from the throngs who flocked to see the Chester pageants. But this passion, to maintain itself pure and rich, needed to be fed from a more ethereal height than the scaffold platform. The angels, who waved their gilt wings century after century on those trundling stages, made no advance in individuality or symbolic beauty. That is not so strange. Angels are not easily persuaded to stoop to human acquaintance. Since the days of Ezekiel, or, at latest, of the seer of Patmos, no poet save Dante has looked upon the angels. But the Miracle conception of the Creator need not, one would think, be quite so bad. It is, with few exceptions, either puerile and preposterous, or remote and colourless. It was on Christ and Mary Mother that the ardent devotion of mediævalism lavished itself. It was those gracious Presences that made the pageant scaffold holy. The rude, warm heart of England still throbbed in love and adoration for these, long after the snow-white vesture and crimson shoes had lost significance in familiarity. But none the less the material presentment was slowly chilling that great religious heart. An ascending Christ, whom the angels had to draw up by ropes, could not hold fealty forever. The modern world refused allegiance, and the pageant scaffold fell. For, while the Middle Ages were the ages of art, as they were the ages of faith, it was a romantic art, in certain features a barbaric art, unguided, untaught; and it was a blind faith, bowed in ignorant obedience before the authority of Rome. The Renascence drew back the curtain which had so long hidden the classic world, and, as the severely ordered beauty of its noble art became revealed, the wild, joyous, youthful riot of the mediæval blood was awed and tamed. But it is not enough to say that the refined taste of the Renascence period laughed down the crude old dramas. The Reformation frowned them down. They had rendered religious service. Who can doubt it? They had impressed one aspect of the Christian revelation, but it was time that another aspect should claim attention. In the main the Mysteries were faithful to the watchword : "God is love." That patient figure of the buffeted, taunted, crucified Christ, to curse and insult answering not again, turning His cheek to the smiter, uttering with dying lips a prayer for His tormentors, — how it tutored, mastered, transformed, exalted the fierce Northmen, who, for five centuries and more, gazed upon the enacted tragedy! The lesson, even yet, is far from learned. The victories of force, the flash of animal courage, still appeal to English instinct more promptly than the victories of gentleness, the glow of moral heroism. Yet the Gothic blood was under schooling for this very fault all through the Middle Ages. The Griseldas, the Nutbrown Maids, the Fair Annies united with saint-lore and martyr-lore, and with the constant spectacle of sad-robed monks, grasping missal and rosary instead of sword and bridle-rein, of barefoot friars, of nuns and penitents, to stamp the fundamental tenet of Christianity deep upon the rugged Teutonic heart. Central in that mediæval object-teaching stood the white, golden-haloed figure, about whom all the pageants of the Miracle Cycle sprang up, but the occasional false note, as the pageant of the Harrowing of Hell, with the overthrow of the Fiend by Christ in furious wrestle, shows too clearly that the native paganism in the beholders was not completely melted, that the old war-song of *Beowulf* still echoed in the air.

Nevertheless, the prevailing tendency of the New Testament pageants was to show the beauty of meekness, the grace of forgiveness, the redemptive power of love. But the text "God is love" is not the only key-word of the Christian religion. It was said again: "God is a Spirit, and they that worship Him must worship Him in spirit." Because this word had been wellnigh forgotten by mediæval Catholicism, Protestantism swept over northern Europe like a fresh, strong, purifying wave. And none of the products of the Middle Ages had sinned more grievously against spirituality than the Miracle Plays, with their God in a gilt peruke and their Christ in red slippers, their insistence upon the physical agonies of Gethsemane and Calvary, their palpable Immaculate Conceptions and Resurrections. The

Reformation, hungering and thirsting after the
Divine, could not brook the triviality, the grossness,
the falseness, of the old religious stage. It swept
the land clear of it. It destroyed records and manuscripts, — all with the same headstrong vehemence,
the same impetuosity of indignation with which it
tore down the long-worshipped images of the Virgin, rifled the shrines of the saints, scraped away
frescoes, and mutilated carvings, and crushed into
myriad fragments the enchanted windows, which
not all the wizardry of modern art and science can
replace. The Miracle Plays but went the way of
all who have served their time, who have done
with much of evil more of good, and whose mission
is ended. Their opportunity was a large one.
Jusserand exclaims : —

"Cinq à six cents ans de popularité ! Quelle pièce de
théâtre occupa si longtemps la scène ! Est-il une seule
œuvre littéraire qui soit restée tant de siècles vivante, au
grand soleil, avant d'aller tristement jouir de l'immortalité, a
l'ombre des bibliothèques des savants ? Au premier abord,
nous avons peine à comprendre aujourd'hui cette admiration
universelle, car enfin ce n'etait pas seulement la foule des
marchands et des laboureurs qui allait voir Pilate et Noé ;
c'était toute la ville et même toute la nation, les gens du
peuple, les bourgeois, les nobles, les clercs, et le roi."

And with all other service rendered by the Miracle
Cycles, they served the Elizabethan drama well.

They not only bequeathed to it scope and freedom, great constructive principles, reality of characterisation, and intensity of passion, but they paved the way for its reception. They made England a nation of actors, a nation of theatre-lovers, a nation of deep dramatic cravings, who would be content with no such learned and elegant trifling as amused the court and university, but cried out for range, for earnestness, for life. To follow the history of feudal England through a series of plays was little for those whose grandsires had followed the history of mankind. Londoners had looked already on a more heart-moving tragedy than *Hamlet.*

CHAPTER V.

MORALITIES.

THE very word is like a yawn. The most un-
daunted stormer of the Miracle Cycle, repellent fortress that it looks to be, may be forgiven if he
blenches before the onset of this ragged regiment,
if he draws a sigh or two before brushing the cob-
webs from odd volumes of Dodsley and the Shakespeare Society Publications, and settling down to
read from top to bottom of his Morality list. Per-
severe to the end he may, but let no man count his
nods. My own experience tends to the conclusion
that the easiest way to read a Morality is with a
book-mark at the last page. When the jaded brain,
for nothing tires like stupidity, is capable of no
other delight, there is still a shamefaced pleasure in
counting the leaves that intervene before that blessed
goal. One rises at last, gray of visage and glum of
mood, with a sense of dust in the nostrils, and discovers in surprise that all through this irrevocable
morning of poring over tedious pages, there has

been summer out of doors,—silver rain in fragrant woodlands and chirp of hidden birds. How could these old plays manage it to be so dry and tuneless, with human life in its richness and sweetness all about them? It must be because in these is committed the cardinal sin of literature,—the forsaking of the concrete for the abstract. The magnificent criminals, as always,.go scot-free. Spenser and Bunyan range the world at will. But these petty offenders, the Morality authors, must feel the weight of our just indignation. They have bored us, their gentle readers, who are not personified qualities nor any fashion of psychological figments, but human beings, living creatures, responding with sympathetic comprehension to Joseph, to Balaam, even to their asses, as we can never respond to Mundus and Studious Desire and Honest Recreation. The Moralities, as a rule, are successful only in failure. When the abstract blunders into the concrete, when the moral play clumsily slips over into human comedy or tragedy, it is possible to become interested. That flimsy garment of flesh and blood worn by Hycke-Scorner endears the vagabond, though even he is ridiculously suggestive of Hawthorne's Feathertop, "There it stood,—poor devil of a contrivance that it was!—with only the thinnest vesture of human similitude about it, through which was evident the stiff, rickety, incongruous, faded, tattered, good-for-nothing patchwork of its substance, ready to sink in a heap upon the floor, as conscious of its own unworthiness to be erect."

The Moralities, everywhere far more restricted in date than the Miracles, appeared in England a century later than in France, where they were of a lighter and less sectarian description. Passing by the lost Pater Noster Play and Creed Play of York, these fourteenth century dramas which seem to have had the essential quality of Moralities, we find that the English Moral Plays, which apparently rose in the East Midland district, where the Norman influence was always strong, were in vogue from the second quarter of the fifteenth century on through the earlier half of the reign of Elizabeth, their tendency being to become less and less dramatic, and more and more controversial, usually in support of the Reformed Faith. As to their origin there are sundry theories, each of which seems to contain some portion of the truth. If we cannot believe, with Warton, that the Moralities are the direct offspring of the processional pageants, we should, nevertheless, be slow to affirm that the popular familiarity with allegorical figures, as used in pageantry, had no bearing on the conception of this new group of *dramatis personæ*. The sacred procession has, indeed, so strong a hold on the populace that it still survives in regions where the Mystery and Morality are at present almost or entirely unknown, as in districts of Italy, Switzerland, Spain, and conspicuously in Mexico and Central America. If Collier's holding, that the Moralities were gradually developed out of the Mysteries through the workings of a natural desire for variety, which, having first suggested the elaboration of minor characters in the Scriptural dramas, led also, in course of time, to the introduction of personifications, can hardly be accepted in its entirety, yet we may at least admit that the earlier Moralities were modelled upon the Mysteries, especially in manner of presentation, and without this antecedent drama assuredly would never have existed as the plays they are. We may grant to Ward that the figurative element in Scripture and the allegorising tendencies of the current literature, especially in France, were potent in furthering these allegorical church plays, but while so deciding with Ward, as against Collier, that the Morality, although never independent of the Mystery, was not derived from it in any onward process of evolution, the way is open for us to assent to Symonds' proposition that the Morality holds to the Mystery the relation of a barren and abortive side growth.

"We might compare it to one of those imperfect organisms which have long since perished in the struggle for existence, but which interest the physiologist, both as indicating an effort after development upon a line which proved to be the weaker, and also as containing within itself evidences of the structure which finally succeeded."

We may well be on our guard, however, against accepting too readily Symonds' plausible suggestion that the Morality connects itself with the later and degenerate Mystery, in which a single personage, as Saul or Mary Magdalene, and no longer the human race, is protagonist. In the earlier Moralities it is this very *Genus Humanum*, variously personified, that stands as centre of the drama. The tendency to contract and to individualise is with the Moralities, as with the Mysteries, characteristic of a secondary stage. Nor should we commit ourselves rashly to Jusserand's theory that the Moralities represent the intellectual side of mediævalism, its scholastic philosophy, and its infantile science, as an offset to the religious side of mediævalism, represented by the Miracle Play. The flaw here apparently lies in Jusserand's selection of characteristic Moralities. England has so-called Moralities dealing with morals and subjects spiritual, and other so-called Moralities dealing with subjects intellectual. Apart from the name itself, which should be sufficient, it would seem, to determine which of these varieties is the original and genuine Moral Play, a comparison of extant Moralities makes evident the order of development.

On all dramatic questions, deference is due to the opinion of the laborious German critic, Klein, who lays stress upon the Vice as the significant link between the Mystery and the Morality. The derivation of the name Vice has been much disputed, as if in very perversity of criticism, for what objection, save its simplicity, can be brought against the obvious etymology? The Vice is always vicious, "a flippant and persistent elf of evil," as Symonds styles him, but the peculiar form of evil which he represents is varied to suit the character of the play. He is Shift, Ambition, Infidelity; he is Sin, Inclination, Hypocrisy, and he is Haphazard, Hardy-dardy, and Sir Nichol Newfangle. Shakespeare and Ben Jonson both speak of him as Iniquity, but the Vice and Iniquity were sometimes distinct characters. In the play of *Histriomastix*, 1610, occurs the stage direction: " Enter a roaring Devil with *the Vice* on his back, *Iniquity* in one hand, and *Juventus* in the other."

For although the Vice of the Moralities derived from the Devil of the Mysteries and fathered the Shakespearian fool, yet even as the Mysteries and Moralities lived on side by side, the Vice did not at once banish the Devil from the religious stage. Judging less from the few extant English Moralities than from hints here and there in later Elizabethan literature, the Vice was often to be found in attend-

ance upon this harassed fiend, whom he teased and
tormented with a thousand nimble pranks, until the
roguish servitor met his appropriate end of being
carried off to hell upon the Devil's back, — unless,
indeed, as in the play of *King Darius*, the Vice
scampered down to hell of his own accord to escape
the society of the Virtues. Sometimes the Vice,
whose proper office it was to instigate the hero of
the play to wickedness, took it upon him to protect
his victim from the premature assaults of the Devil,
but more frequently this nimble Harlequin seemed
to plague the clumsy, howling fiend from sheer
wantonness of mischief. He liked to leap upon
the Devil's shaggy shoulders, belabouring them
with his famous wooden sword until the exasper-
ated monster roared again, to the exceeding joy
of the audience. The function of the Vice thus
being that of chief comedian, he ordinarily wore
the gay, parti-coloured dress of the domestic fool, —
a favourite figure, at about the middle of the sixteenth century, in the halls of the English nobility.
This mere circumstance of the dress doubtless had
no small share in bringing about the transformation
of the Vice, who, on the Morality stage, was little
better than a buffoon, regaling the audience with
capers, jugglery, and verbal quiddities, into the
Feste and Touchstone of the Shakespearian drama.
But occasionally the plot required the Vice to ap-

pear as a gallant, or take some other part for
which the fool-dress was unsuitable, and so his
costume became subject to almost as many changes
as his name. This rôle of the Vice, so ingenious
a mode of relieving what must have been otherwise
the almost insupportable tedium of the Morality
Plays, was unknown to the French stage. In this
their own creation the English rejoiced hugely, and
it left a deep impression upon the popular memory,
as various allusions of the Jacobean drama, especially of the Jonsonian drama, bear witness.

But Klein holds the Vice, with all the other sins
this skipping antic has to answer for, responsible for
the final triumph of the Moralities over the Mysteries. The Devil of the Miracle Play was no theological abstraction, but a dramatic character of
originally heroic proportions, Lucifer, the Archangel
Fallen. So long as the Devil appeared upon the
Morality stage, in however uncouth and preposterous a form, something of this original reality still
invested him, differentiating him sharply from the
shadowy throng of allegorical personages. But presently the Vice, with his incessant badgering, hunted
the Devil off the boards, actually worried him from
the stage where he had ruled for centuries, usurped
his place, and degraded his primal significance into
tomfooleries. This final substitution of the Vice
for the Devil robbed the Morality of its one shred

of dramatic substance. Thenceforth the Moral Play was dramatically a thing of naught, tending directly toward didacticism and polemics. It was in itself a retrogression from the Mystery, although opening the way, in its escape from sacred material and from set rôles, for originality and dramatic freshness.

The prevailing opinion of our assembly of critics would seem to be that the development of the Moralities from the Miracles was superficial, not fundamental. Moral Plays found their suggestion in the allegorising tendencies of the times and took form under the influence of the elder drama, varied by the impulse toward dramatic novelty, and also by the impulse toward didactic completeness, in that the Mysteries, as Mr. Pollard has pointed out, gave only the historical teaching of the Church, not her ethical and sacramental holdings.

The classification of the extant English Moralities has been a dark matter. Even the patient, much-perusing Mr. Collier left them in a clutter. But Mr. Pollard has recently brought a lantern into this lumber attic, making a valuable distinction between the longer, earlier Moral Plays, "concerned with issues that touch the whole of human nature," and the Moral Interludes, setting forth only a portion of the human warfare, and so brief as to serve for presentation between the courses of luxurious banquets. The Moral Interludes fall again into two classes, the

first warning youth against profligacy and false
theology, the second against intellectual sloth and
false science.

It would probably not be too much in the way of
theatrical excitement, if we should attend the performance of a representative play in each of these
three divisions. Transporting ourselves back to the
unhappy reign of Henry VI., we join the merry-
making throng of villagers, who, for this once forget-
ful of wars in France and miseries at home, are
pressing in from various East Midland hamlets to
the central market town, where, as criers a week
ago announced throughout the neighbourhood, to-day
is to be exhibited "on the grene in ryall aray" the
new play known as the *Castell of Perseverance.* It
puzzles peasant brains to comprehend how it can
be a play when there are no glittering pageant car-
riages rolling from street to street, but nevertheless
the rustics hasten with the clerks and gentles to
secure good places on the borders of the grassy
common. Within the green enclosure rises a temporary erection which bears some rough resemblance
to a Norman hold. It is propped up from the
ground with blocks, so disclosing a bed beneath it.
The audience, understanding that the chief actor,
Genus Humanum, is concealed beneath the bed,
waiting his cue, regard this piece of domestic archi-
tecture with lively curiosity. Grouped about the

castle, at a respectful distance, are five stationary scaffolds : the respective stages of the World, the Flesh, the Devil, Covetousness, and God.

The three first grandees, the World, the Flesh, and the Devil, appear each on his own platform, with braggart speeches. Then little Genus Humanum, the white baptismal cloth thrown over his baby head, crawls out from under the couch. This unfortunate child, not yet a day old, although a fluent declaimer, is at once assailed by a good angel from the right and a bad angel from the left. Each presses his guardianship upon the bewildered infant, who between them wavers "as wynde in watyr." But the bad angel, offering gold, which tips the scale, quiets all fears for the future by the suggestion : —

> " With the werld thou mayst be bold,
> Tyl thou be sexty wynter hold ;
> Wanne thi nose waxit cold
> Thanne mayst thou drawe to goode."

The poor baby declares for the bad angel, and the good angel is left wringing his hands and chanting a lament. Genus Humanum, grown to youth's estate, visits the scaffolds of the World, the Flesh, and the Devil, making such disreputable acquaintances as Pleasure, Folly, Slander, and the Seven Deadly Sins. The good angel is " sobbing sore " over these wandering courses, when Shrift and Confession revive his courage for a fresh appeal to Genus Humanum, who, now in the fullness of manhood, admits his error, forsakes his sins, and begs for protection from his enemies. He is accordingly housed for safe-keeping in the " Castell of Perseverance," —

> " a precyous place,
> Fful of vertu and of grace."

Slander hurries with the news up to the scaffolds of the World and the Flesh. The Seven Deadly Sins, léd by the Devil, storm the castle, the Virtues beating them back with roses, emblems of the Saviour's Passion. This storming scene calls out unbounded enthusiasm from the audience, many of whom have served in the French wars. But wrinkled old Covetousness softly descends from his chilly scaffold in the northeast and, by the promise of a thousand marks, lures Genus Humanum, now an old man, out from his sure fortress. The money, which its new owner is forbidden to give to the poor or to the Church, is hidden in the ground, until Death appears on the scene, when the World claims the treasure for his own. Genus Humanum, terrified and wretched, is smitten down by Death, and his trembling soul mounts the eastern scaffold, God's scaffold, for judgment. The four daughters of God, fair sister-angels, gather about him. Truth, clad in "sad grene," recounts his misdeeds. Justice, robed in burning red, would refuse him salvation.

"Lete hym drynke as he brewyit."

But Peace, garmented all in black, urges that if any sinner be left unreconciled to God, her mourning has no end, and white-vested Mercy pleads the Divine Passion. So, as always in these old Moralities, pity and pardon close the drama. The sin-stained soul is purified and blessed. Genus Humanum, after all his earthly waywardness and weakness, is saved by grace of God.

In a play like this we have no longer the history of the human race, conceived from the Christian point of view, but of the individual soul. To portray the life of man from the cradle to beyond the grave, even to the fixing of his eternal destiny, is no mean endeavour. To depict this human life as the prize for which heavenly spirits wage continual warfare against the lords of hell has in it something of dramatic salt. But the characters are empty masks, and the essential absurdity in a hero who must be represented at the varying stages from boyhood to old age — indeed, to post-mortem spiritual existence — is a difficulty not to be overcome.

The Castell of Perseverance, probably based, more or less directly, upon a French original, is one of the Macro Moralities, a group of three old plays which derive their alliterative title from having once been in the possession of a certain Mr. Macro. The second of these, entitled by Collier *Mind, Will, and Understanding*, and by Furnivall *A Morality of Wisdom Who is Christ*, is also a play of scope and dignity. Wisdom, resplendent in purple, gold, and ermine, opens the play with a declaration of His divinity. Anima, the Human Soul, white-robed and beautiful, kneels and beseeches His love. After long theological discussion, the Five Wits enter as five innocent maidens. and are bidden by Wisdom preserve their whiteness and keep themselves un-spotted from the world. Mind, Will, and Under-standing share in the purity and in the exhortation. Then enters Lucifer, wearing under his devil's dress the suit of a dandy. He corrupts the Mind, the Understanding, and the Will, and the Soul grows foul with the foulness of these her ministers. Evil creatures in fantastic costumes troop about them and dance the Devil's dance. Wisdom returns to find the Anima He has loved hideously transformed, but in the light of His presence Mind, Will, and Understanding return to the truth, and Anima is restored to beauty.

The third of the Macro Moralities, entitled *Mankind*, still waits an editor. Again is delineated the struggle between Mercy and Mischief for the soul of Mankind, who, at the outset, is obedient to Mercy and disposed, as befits the son of Adam, to ply the spade with diligence. But idle and vicious companions get by trickery this honourable implement away from him and lead him so far astray that he is on the point of hanging himself, when Mercy comes to his rescue. Mankind's own account of his fallen state is too pithy to be passed over : —

" My name is Mankynde : I have my composycyon
    Of a body and of a soull, of condycyon contrarye :
Betwyx the tweyn ys a grett dyvisyon ;
    He that shulde be sojecte now he hath the victory.
Thys ys to me a lementable story,
    To se my flesch of my soull to have governaunce :
Wher the good wyff ys master, the good man may be
    sory."

Mundus et Infans, another of these ancient Moralities, would serve as an extended commentary on the famous oration of the melancholy Jaques. The infant, whom the cynical old bachelor of Arden so ungraciously describes as

    " Mewling and puking in the nurse's arms,"

is here playfully styled Daliance by his fond mother. Little Daliance speedily grows into mischievous Wanton, who fully shares the objections of his Shakespearian successor to school-going, being, indeed, the liveliest youngster that ever robbed an orchard or spied a sparrow's nest.

> " I can daunce and also skyppe,
> I can playe at the chery pytte,
> And I can wystell you a fytte."

But top-spinning, run-away Wanton becomes in
short time the fickle lover, Lust-and-Liking,

> " All game and gle,
> All myrthe and melodye."

Soon his one and twenty years are spent, and his
name is altered to Manhood.   Hitherto Mundus
has had undisputed ascendancy over this reckless
Infans, but now Conscience presents himself, meeting with a somewhat discouraging reception.

Manhode. Conscyence ! what the devyll man is he ?
Conscyence. Syr, a techer of the spyrytualete.
Manhode. Spyrytualete ! what the devyll may that be ?

Folly makes his way more readily with young Manhood, bestowing upon him the new appellation of
Shame, but Conscience appeals to Perseverance for
help, and by the time the hero has reached the
title of Age, shifting

> " Into the lean and slipper'd pantaloon,"

he proves tractable to holy counsel, and is finally
dubbed Repentance.

A sterner drama is *Everyman*, deservedly the
most popular of these earlier Moralities. Dr. Henri
Logemann has lately shown, by publishing the two in
parallel columns, that the English Morality is taken

from a Dutch play, *Elkerlyck*, probably by Petrus Dorlandus. A Latin version also is extant.

Death, God's "mighty messenger," summons Everyman to the long pilgrimage. Bribes, tears, entreaties are all of no avail. The one grace the grim messenger will grant is permission for Everyman to take with him on that mysterious journey such of his friends as may consent to bear him company. Everyman applies to Fellowship, who is ready to follow on to feast or frolic, but flees away at the mention of Death. Kindred lamely excuses himself as having the cramp in his toe, and Gold, the tempter and destroyer, exults in Everyman's distress. Good Deeds would gladly serve him, but she lies helpless, crushed under the weight of his sins, until her sister Knowledge guides him to Confession, who shrives him from his guilt. Then Good Deeds is able to rise and accompany Everyman as he paces fearfully toward the church-yard. Beauty, Strength, Discretion, and Five Wits attend him for a space, but shudder at the sight of the grave and fall away. Good Deeds alone, though partaking of their dread, stands firm.

"Shorte our ende and mynysshe our payne,"

she entreats, and they go down into the grave together, an angel overhead singing welcome to the passing soul.

A fragment of an old Morality, somewhat kindred in theme, has recently been discovered in Ireland. Here man figures as the King of Life, with Health and Strength for his attendant knights. Confident in their support, he sends Mirth, his messenger, to challenge Death. The proud challenger is slain, but his soul is rescued from hell by the intercession of Mary.

These two latter Moralities, it should be noticed, do not set forth progressively the course of human life, but they gather up into the last inevitable hour the power and significance of all that has gone before. A comparatively late Morality of the ampler type, *Nature*, written by Henry Medwall, chaplain to Cardinal Morton, early in the reign of Henry VII., follows again the elder fashion, depicting man as wavering between allegiance to Reason and to Sensuality. The Deadly Sins change their names to deceive him, Gluttony, for instance, presenting himself as Good Fellowship, and Covetousness as Worldly Policy. Age, at last, dismisses the Vices and welcomes the Virtues, and this play, like the rest, ends with a promise of salvation.

It is clear that these early Moralities bear a supplementary relation to the Miracle Cycles. It is Christian experience added to Christian theology, and Christian experience in its full scope and development. There is no Vice in these original

Moralities, and, of course, no trace of the Reformed Faith. It is not until we reach the reign of Henry VIII. that we can expect to find the drama taking up arms for Protestantism.

The Moral Interludes bring us fairly into Tudor times. If we would see one of these degenerate Moralities performed, we must take our way not to the open green, but to some vaulted banquet-hall. A group of strolling actors, only four in number, sheltering themselves under the name of my Lord Cardinal's Players, have scented the feast and come begging for leave to show an interlude. There are tawdry stage effects carried in bundles upon their shoulders ; there is a boy for the woman's parts, and there is a choice to be had of some half dozen stale Moralities, as well known to audience as to players, though the verses are frayed and tattered by time, like the wigs and mantles. It is a zealously Protestant household, and the voice of the company is for *Lusty Juventus*. There are various halts and hitches in the performance, for there are nine parts to be carried by the four players, and, if any article of the wardrobe is mislaid, if Hypocrisy cannot put his hand upon his dancing pumps, or if Satan has forgotten his horns, there is nothing for the audience to do but sit and crack nuts until the boy has fetched the missing properties from the players' squalid lodging. But despite these occasional embarrassments, the little troupe plays with such vivacity and spirit that the spectators never once suspect how dull and un-dramatic their chosen interlude really is.

After a didactic prologue, advocating severity in the training of youth, Lusty Juventus enters, singing a song which is much too good for the play.

> "In a herber green, asleep where as I lay,
>   The birds sang sweet in the middes of the day ;
>   I dreamed fast of mirth and play :
>   In youth is pleasure, in youth is pleasure.
>
> "Methought I walked still to and fro,
>   And from her company I could not go ;
>   But when I waked, it was not so :
>   In youth is pleasure, in youth is pleasure.
>
> "Therefore my heart is sorely pight
>   Of her alone to have a sight,
>   Which is my joy and heart's delight :
>   In youth is pleasure, in youth is pleasure."

Two solemn graybeards, Good Counsel and Knowledge, take this young trifler in hand, and, by dint of prolonged catechism and exhortation, make a Protestant of him. Rejoicing over this hopeful conversion, the two sermonisers withdraw, dutifully followed by Lusty Juventus, whereupon the Devil, with a roar and a bound, takes possession of the stage. He complains that, while the old people remain good Papists, the young are all flocking to the new faith.

> "They will not believe, they plainly say,
>   In old traditions and made by men,
>   But they will live, as the Scripture teacheth them."

The Devil bethinks himself, in this perplexity, of his son Hypocrisy, who comes capering upon the boards with many a nimble antic, singing a rattling ditty about the shams of the Romish Church :—

> "Holy days, holy fastings,
>   Holy twitchings, holy tastings,
>   Holy visions and sights,
>   Holy wax, holy lead,
>   Holy water, holy bread,
>   To drive away sprites,
>   Holy fire, holy palm,
>   Holy oil, holy cream,
>   And holy ashes also ;
>   Holy brooches, holy rings,
>   Holy kneeling, holy censings,
>   And a hundred trim-trams mo."

Hypocrisy engages to recapture Juventus, and, encountering the poor lad before his Protestantism has had time to dry, by flattery and ridicule wins him over. Fellowship, in dishevelled finery, struts upon the stage, followed by the boy of the troupe in the guise of a woman, Abominable Living. The four players, the entire company being now in action, make merry together and sing another blithe and buoyant song.

" Why should not youth fulfil his own mind,
　　As the course of nature doth him bind ?
　　Is not everything ordained to do his kind ?
　　　　Report me to you, report me to you.

" Do not the flowers spring fresh and gay,
　　Pleasant and sweet in the month of May ?
　　And when their time cometh, they fade away.
　　　　Report me to you, report me to you."

The stage is left empty for a few minutes, while one of the players dresses for Good Counsel, who presently appears, much cast down over the defection of Juventus. This young backslider, entering with an air of cheerful impudence, is soon browbeaten into repentance and falls prone upon the floor in extreme distress of mind. Merciful Promises raises the penitent, who addresses a long and edifying exhortation to the audience. This well over, the players drop upon their knees and pray for the king, the nobles, and the magistrates. The guests politely applaud the interlude, while the lord of the feast tosses a few gold pieces to the players, who fall to scrambling for them in the rushes.

These Moral Interludes were not all of Protestant complexion. A Papist household would regale itself with *Hycke-Scorner*, or, if *Hycke-Scorner* was deemed old-fashioned, with its more elegant recast, *The Interlude of Youth. Hycke-Scorner* is a curiosity in the allegorical drama, for there is nothing dramatic about

it and little enough of allegory. There are six
characters, three good and three bad. The former
class is made up of Pity, Contemplation, and Perseverance, sociable old worthies, who take occasion
to deplore, among other lamentable matters, that
which the nineteenth century is inclined to claim
as her particular discovery, — the sufferings of the
poor : —

> " I have herde many men complayne pyteously ;
> They saye they be smyten with the swerde of poverty,
> In every place where I do go :
> Fewe frendes povertee dooth fynde,
> And these ryche men ben unkynde."

The dissolute young madcaps are, in this case,
Frewyll, Imagynacyon, and Hycke-Scorner, this last
an extensive traveller, who has even journeyed to

> " the londe of Rumbelowe,
> Thre myl out of hell."

But although he gives his name to the play,
Hycke-Scorner is the least important character in
the cast, no one taking the trouble to convert him,
while his two wild companions, by the exertion of
the venerable preachers, are duly provided with new
names and robes of righteousness.

The Interlude of Youth, conjectured to belong to
the reign of Mary, is a better piece of work. Riot,
modelled after Imagination in the earlier play, takes

the part of the Vice, and, seconded by Pride and Lady Lechery, seduces Youth, who is rescued in the end by Charity and Humility. The author borrowed much of his language and something of his characterisation from *Hycke-Scorner*, but he was alive to the necessity of a central character and a consistent theme.

The second class of Moral Interludes, the Interludes whose main concern is science rather than ethics, has two notable examples extant in *The Nature of the Four Elements* and Redford's *Wyt and Science*. The first of these was written within the next generation after the discovery of America, and suggests the bewildering variety of new ideas into which the human mind was eagerly inquiring. The prologue is spoken by a Messenger, who laments that all learning is sealed up in Latin books, and that English literature amounts to nothing but idle fantasies and ballads

"of love or other matter not worth a mite."

Nature enters and delivers to open-eared Humanity a lecture in astronomy, upon which Studious Desire proceeds to examine him. Sensuality comes to the relief of the fasting student and carries him off to the tavern, where he is refreshed for a lesson in geography, imparted by a travelled gentleman known as Experience. Ignorance breaks in with a song and a dance, and Nature comes to see how Humanity is getting on, reminding him gravely that while mirth and feasting are not altogether amiss, he should devote himself principally to study, — a right Renascence conclusion.

We will not venture before the stage of this formidable drama, with its "many proper points of philosophy natural, and of divers strange effects and causes," although the author fairly buttonholes us with wistful importunity, protesting that the interlude can be played in an hour and a half, or "if ye list, ye may leave out much of the sad matter, as the Messenger's part, and some of Nature's part, and some of Experience's part, and yet the matter will depend conveniently, and then it will not be past three-quarters of an hour in length."

But if we must see one of these educational Moralities, let it be *Wyt and Science*, written some score of years before the birth of Shakespeare. I think we shall not go astray if we enter the many-gabled, half-timbered edifice of one of Edward VI.'s Free Grammar Schools, where for the afternoon Ovid and Seneca are thrown aside, and the ruddy young Britons, with gleeful excitement and stir, are making ready to perform, for the delectation of their admiring kith and kin, Master John Redford's popular interlude. At one end of the handsome Tudor hall, with its latticed windows and

oak-raftered roof, a temporary stage has been roughly
knocked together. Down the length of the hall below the stage are benches and stools for the stout
burghers and the merry wives, and everywhere
boys are thick as pepper, encamped in phalanxes
upon the floor, flattened against the walls, even
perched on the massive cross-beams of the roof.
A blue-eyed English lad, dressed in flowing gown
and long white beard for Reason, steps forth upon
the stage, and in a voice appropriately tremulous
confides to the audience that his daughter Science
and youthful Wit have fallen in love, and that he
himself is, on the whole, disposed to bless the banns,
enunciating the sound old doctrine : —

> " Where pertyes together be enclynde
> By gyftes of graces to love ech other,
>   There let them joyne the tone wyth the toother."

It is the head boy who comes on in the coveted
rôle of Wit, and all the little fellows on the floor
twist about impatiently through the preliminary
dialogue, until the giant Tediousness, an overgrown
young bully who is the terror of the lower forms,
strides out, yawning prodigiously, upon the stage,
in an ill-fitting suit of rusty mail, with a battered
helmet on his head. Too-impetuous Wit, without
waiting for " wepens of science," and deserted by
Study, who pleads a headache, rushes forward to

the encounter, but is forthwith smitten down and killed by the giant. Wit's mother, in the audience, being "a very simplicity oman," can hardly keep back her tears. But Tediousness, with a triumphant flourish of his mace, stalks off the stage, and the buxom lass Honest Recreation, aided by other kindly nurses, rubs and chafes the fallen hero until he rises to his feet as well as ever. Reason enters to rebuke Wit for his rashness. The fickle young wooer, sulking at this, proposes to give over the courtship of difficult Lady Science, and makes love on the spot to Honest Recreation, who sets him to dancing in test of his merit. Meanwhile that disreputable slattern, Idleness, enters, lazily taking seat upon the stage, and Wit, when he is tired of dancing, flings himself down with his head in her lap. Honest Recreation, poor girl, flies furiously at Idleness, demanding her lover, and a shrill-tongued quarrel ensues between these rival sweethearts. Both appeal to Wit, Honest Recreation voicing an eloquent defence of athletics, but the naughty boy chooses Idleness, and his wholesome, red-cheeked hoyden departs in tears. Treacherous Idleness rocks Wit asleep in her lap, and then whistles for the booby Ignorance, who comes in "deckt lyke a very asse." If there was a Holofernes in that assembly, doubtless he muttered under his breath: "O thou monster Ignorance, how

deformed dost thou look!" And, in truth, Ignorance is such a superlative blockhead that the lad
who takes the part blushes behind his mask.

Then comes the most diverting spelling lesson
on record.

Idlenes. Say thy lesson, foole.

Ingnorance. Upon my thummes?

   Id. Ye, upon thy thummes; ys not there thy name?

Ing. Yeas.

   Id. Go to, than spell me that same.

       Wher was thou borne?

Ing. Chwas i-bore in Ingland, mother sed.

   Id. In Ingland?

Ing. Yea.

   Id. And what's half Ingland?

       Heeres ing and heeres land, whats tys?

Ing. Tys my thum!

   Id. Thy thum? yng, horeson, ing, ing!

Ing. Yng, yng, yng, yng.

    *   *   *   *   *

   Id. Say no, foole, say no.

Ing. Noo, noo, noo, noo, noo!

   Id. Go to, put together yng.

Ing. Yng.

   Id. No!

Ing. Noo.

   Id. Forth now! what sayth the dog?

Ing. Dog barke.

   Id. Dog barke? dog ran, horeson, dog ran?

Ing. Dog ran, horson, dog ran, dog ran!

Id. Put together ing.

Ing. Yng.

Id. No.

Ing. Noo.

Id. Ran.

Ing. Ran.

Id. Foorth now, what seyth the goose?

Ing. Lag, lag.

Id. Hys, horson, hys !

Ing. Hys, hys, s—s—s—s.

Id. Go to, put together yng.

Ing. Ing.

Id. No.

Ing. Noo.

Id. Ran.

Ing. Ran.

Id. Hys.

Ing. Hys, s—s—s—s—s—s.

Id. Now, who is a good boy?

Ing. I, I, I, I, I, I.

Id. Go to, put together ing.

Ing. Ing.

Id. No.

Ing. Noo.

Id. Ran.

Ing. Ran.

Id. His.

Ing. Hys — s, s, s, s, s.

Id. I.

Ing. I.

Id. Ing, no, ran, his, I.

Ing. Ing, no, ran, hys—s—s—s.

Id. I.

Ing. I.

Id. Ing.

Ing. Ing.

Id. Foorth.

Ing. Hys—s—s—s.

Id. Ye, no, horeson, no !

Ing. Noo, noo, noo, noo.

Id. Ing, no.

Ing. Ing, noo.

Id. Forth now.

Ing. Hys, s—s—s—s.

Id. Yet agayne ; ran, horeson, ran, ran.

Ing. Ran, horson, ran, ran.

Id. Ran say.

Ing. Ran say.

Id. Ran, horson.

Ing. Ran, horeson.

Id. Ran.

Ing. Ran.

Id. Ing, no, ran.

Ing. Ing, no, ran.

Id. Foorth, now, what sayd the goose ?

Ing. Dog barke.

Id. Dog barke?   Hys, horson, hys—s—s—s—s—s.

Ing. Hys—s—s—s—s—s—s.

Id. I.

Ing. Ing,—no,—ran, hys, I.

*   *   *   *   *   *

Id. How sayst, now, foole, is not there thy name ?

Ing. Yea.

Id. Well than, can me that same.
   What hast thow lernd?
Ing. Ich can not tell.

As a reward for his exertions, Ignorance, bidden
by Idleness, puts on Wit's fine coat, sent by Science
to her recreant suitor, and helps Idleness slip his
own fool's dress on Wit. Then the precious pair
withdraw, leaving Wit, in his uncouth attire, sleeping on the stage. Science enters with her goodly
train, Worship, Riches, Fame, and Favour. She is
chaperoned by her mother Experience. Wit awakes
and has the assurance to present himself to Science
as her "owne deere lover" and ask for a kiss, but
no one knows him disguised as he is in the ugly
hood, with its long ears, and shaggy coat of Ignorance. Flouted and forsaken, he beholds himself in
a mirror and realises his disgrace. Shame enters,
bearing in hand a familiar whip, at sight of which
the boys on the cross-beams curl up their legs, feeling
a retrospective sting. Wit begs off from his flogging,
meekly suffers the reproaches of Reason, submits
to the schooling of Instruction and goes forth,
this time fully equipped, to give battle once more
to Tediousness, whom he flatly overthrows, amidst
thunders of applause from the boys of the lower
forms, and brings back the gaint's head, or helmet,
upon his "sword of comfort" cent him by Lady
Science. With responsive singing the bridal parties

meet. Wit, now robed in the "gown of knowledge,"
has won his fair lady, and to the mind of the young-
est urchin in the hall a glamour of romance and
chivalry will linger, henceforth and forever, about
even the hardest "questions in his accidence."

What is true of the Miracle Cycles, as regards
authorship, is scarcely less true of the original Moralities, those cumbrous, large, religious *Castells of
Perseverance*, and their like. They had no authors.
They grew, not precisely à la Topsy, but with equal
unconsciousness. They are as truly organic, in their
stratum, as the mediæval epics, Beowulf, the Cid,
the Nibelungen Lied, are in theirs, or as the Gothic
cathedrals are in theirs.

It is a noteworthy fact that during the dreary
fifteenth century, that darkness between two dawns,
when England heard no clear individual voices in
her battle-troubled air, the warm, deep heart of the
people still sang on. It is our ballad century. And
what poetry could be spared from the ballads went
into Mysteries and Moralities. But these later Moral
Interludes yield no such reverberation. They are
plainly the handiwork of one dull rhymster or
another, and the significance, the sense of hoarded
life, is out of them. Yet the Moralities, blind to
the breaking of the bright dramatic day, held on
their antiquated path throughout the reign of Elizabeth. This path, however, tended more and more

toward the new highway of the secular drama. We have two Moralities, even before the Elizabethan date, that in their self-conscious elaboration connect themselves with this later development. They are both the work of professional poets, — men of power, too, although the diamond of genius is somewhat in the rough. In *Magnyfycence*, the single survival left to us of Skelton's four plays, the author's characteristic wit and vivacity are smothered in the heavy folds of the allegory, and even Lyndsay's *Satyre of the Thrie Estaitis*, estimable as it is for its earnest advocacy of reform in Church and state, is hardly attractive reading. Both Moralities present the full compass of human experience, though in different fashion. Mankind is personified by Skelton as Magnyfycence, the abstract name of Spenser's King Arthur, and runs through the customary course, passing from the control of the Virtues to that of the Vices, suffering in consequence the blows of Adversity and the visitation of Despair, and rescued at last by such beneficent personages as Good Hope, Sad Circumspection, and the inevitable Perseverance. Lyndsay's dramatic satire is distinctly political, a keen and insistent, if not melodious, voice of the Scottish Reformation. King Humanity, after much wavering between the Virtues and the Vices, gives audience to the Three Estates and a Reform bill is presented.

Of the extant Moralities belonging to the reign of
Elizabeth, some nine seem to have been acted, and,
in most cases, printed, during the boyhood of Shakespeare. The earliest of these, making its title of the
discouraging proverb, *The longer thou livest the more
Foole thou art*, is a continuation of the *Lusty Juventus*
type. The frivolous youth grows to old age in the
drama, however, and is not reclaimed at the end, but
carried off on Confusion's back to the Devil. *Triall
of Treasure*, another Moral Interlude with the note
of the Reformation sounding through it, belaboured
its hearers with a dramatic allegory enforcing the
lesson that worldly wealth is vanity. Inclination,
the Vice of this play, is bridled on the stage by
the "snaffle, called Restraint," the bridle having
come to be almost as distinctive a mark of the
Vice as the striped coat and wooden sword. In
Like wil to like quod the Devel to the Colier we
have a farce built up on allegorical foundation.
Among the alliterative rowdies whom the Vice,
Nichol Newfangle, draws to himself are Ralph
Roister, Tom Tosspot, Piers Pickpurse, and Cuth-
bert Cutpurse. The Collier, who is by no means
a leading character, enters with empty sacks from
a successful market-day, having sold his coals three
pecks to the bushel, and is presented by Nichol
Newfangle to the Devil. Then all three riotously
dance together, in fashion, says the stage direc-

tion, "as evil favoured as may be devised," to the
chorus, —

> " Tom Collier of Croydon hath sold his coals,
>   And made his market to-day ;
>   And now he danceth with the Devil,
>   For like will to like alway."

Such sober personages as Good Fame, Virtuous
Living, God's Promise and Honour strive to reform
this wild company, but without complete success.
Ralph Roister and Tom Tosspot, who have gotten
extremely drunk, repent in season, but Pickpurse
and Cutpurse are betrayed by Nichol Newfangle,
sentenced by Severity, and led off the stage by
Hankin Hangman, with halters about their necks.
Virtuous Life is crowned by Honour, and Nichol
Newfangle, mounting for "a journey to Spain" upon
the Devil's back, is carried down to hell. *The Marriage of Wit and Science* exhibits a technical advance
in its division into acts and scenes, as well as in
versification and diction. It is a clever elaboration
of Redford's allegory already noticed. *New Custome*
is a polemical Interlude on the side of the Reformation, the Puritan Minister, Light of the Gospel,
converting at last the old Papish priest, Perverse
Doctrine. *The Tyde taryeth no Man* also bears the
Reformation impress, but is less of the controversial
temper. *All for Money*, by one Lupton, presents

some surprising effects, which Ben Jonson did not scruple to imitate in *The Poetaster.* Money, taken suddenly ill, vomits Pleasure, who in turn throws up Sin, the Vice, with his wooden dagger. Sin, by the same remarkable process, brings to light Damnation, a terrific figure, and Damnation delivers up the shaggy form of Satan, horns and hoofs and all. This dramatic method may be lacking in delicacy, but the consequences of avarice are certainly made graphic. *The Marriage of Wit and Wisdom* appropriates much scrappy material from its two predecessors on this theme, but introduces various new characters, the vagabond soldiers, Snatch and Catch, old Mother Bee, with her man Lob and her maid Doll, and others pointing unmistakably in the direction of the new comedy. *The Three Ladies of London,* whose names, by the way, are Lucre, Love, and Conscience, was the production of one R. W., and is technically almost in the line of the contemporary secular drama. The author holds to the allegorical framework, however, although admitting a sprinkle of concrete characters, and even so late as 1590 prints an elaborate variation upon his theme in *The Three Lords and Three Ladies of London.* A comparison of the second play with the first would be well worth while, as showing what a London playwright of good ability, with an unfortunate prejudice in favour of Moralities, was learning from the popular stage in those eventful years from 1584 to 1590. The gain in versification is in itself a testimony of the swift advance and irresistible influence of the new dramatic movement. *The Contention between Liberality and Prodigality* was acted before Elizabeth toward the close of her reign, and very likely added a share to her gathering gloom of mind. But Thomas Nabbes lags most conspicuously behind the times with *Microcosmus*, which appeared in 1637.

The progression toward the regular drama traceable through these transitional Moralities is mainly in the line of a growing individuality of characterisation, actual men and women finally appearing side by side with the personified qualities. Progress in dramatic structure is less marked, though apparent, and with the theme remaining abstract, there can be little gain in passion.

The first tentative comedies of the secular drama, apart from the classic imitations, — such comedies as *Jack Juggler*, *Common Conditions*, *Tom Tiler and his Wife*, *The Disobedient Child*, and even *Gammer Gurton's Needle*, still retain Morality features, which are no less apparent in the corresponding attempts of the native drama at secular tragedy, as *Bishop Bale's Kynge Johan*, *The Nice Wanton*, *Cambises*, *Apius and Virginia*, and *The Conflict of Conscience*.

So the great religious drama of England dribbled

out in these miserable hybrids, neither secular nor sacred. But the classic spirit was at work, and although in the end the classic stage became tributary to the Gothic, not its supplanter, it would enter into no compromise with the Vice and his attendant puppets. Indeed, all these later Moralities might well have known better than to be, for Heywood's *Interludes*, genuine farces that they were, had been published in 1532; *Ralph Roister Doister*, clear, secular comedy of the Latin type, had been played before 1551, and *Gorboduc*, true secular tragedy in blank verse, though heavy as lead, by the following year. But life was too rapid in that marvellous second half of the sixteenth century for every man to note carefully what his neighbours had done and were doing, and so we find, under Elizabeth, all the earlier dramatic varieties existing side by side with that Shakespearian stage of which England had hardly become aware. For centuries the Miracle Plays had been preparing the ground, but the Elizabethan Drama itself, under the brilliant sunshine of the Renascence, sprang into so swift and beautiful a blossom that it had already filled the air with its first fresh sweetness before the Elizabethans themselves, even the professed critics of poetry, as Webbe and Puttenham, even the poets of the court, as Sidney and Spenser, were well awake to its existence. Thus we find Miracle Plays, Morality Plays, and Semi-Morality Plays, all three which in dramatic development logically precede the Shakespearian stage, blindly and stupidly pressing on alongside and even overlapping it. It is a rare grace to know when to stop.

APPENDIX.

OUTLINE AND REFERENCES.

Books of General Reference.

Ward, A. W. History of English Dramatic Literature to the Death of Queen Anne.

Collier, J. P. History of English Dramatic Poetry to the Time of Shakespeare, and Annals of the Stage to the Restoration.

Morley, Henry. English Writers.

Symonds, J. A. Shakespeare's Predecessors in the English Drama.

Jusserand, J. J. Le Théâtre en Angleterre.

Sepet, M. Le Drame Chrétien au Moyen Age.

Klein, J. L. Geschichte des Dramas. Vols. XII.–XIII.

Hase, Karl. Das geistliche Schauspiel des Mittelalters. (Translation by A. W. Jackson.)

Ulrici, Hermann. Shakespeare's dramatische Kunst. (Translation in Bohn's Standard Library.)

Reidt, Heinrich. Das geistliche Schauspiel des Mittelalters.

Ebert, Adolf. Jahrbuch für romanische und englische Litteratur. Vol. I.

Ten Brink, Bernhard. Geschichte der englischen Litteratur. Vol. II. (Translation by William Clarke Robinson, Ph. D.)

Warton, Thomas. History of English Poetry.

Hone, William. Ancient Mysteries Described.

Rymer, Thomas. Short View of Tragedy of the Last Age.

Pollard, A. W. English Miracle Plays, Moralities and Interludes. (Introduction and Notes.)

Stoddard, F. H. References for Students of Miracle Plays and
Mysteries. (Univ. of California. Library Bulletin, No. 8.)

A. LATIN PASSION PLAYS AND SAINT PLAYS.

See

Wright, Thomas. Early Mysteries and Latin Poems of the
Twelfth and Thirteenth Centuries.

Pollard, A. W. English Miracle Plays, Moralities and Interludes. Appendix.

Coussemaker, E. de. Drames Liturgiques du Moyen Age.

Du Meril, E. Origines latines du Théâtre moderne.

Froning, R. Das Drama des Mittelalters. Erster Teil. Die
lateinischen Osterfeiern and ihre Entwickelung in Deutsch-
land. Osterspiele. Passionspiele. (Union Deutsche Ver-
lagsgesellschaft.)

B. ENGLISH MIRACLE PLAYS KNOWN TO BE EXTANT.

I. Cycles.

a. YORK PLAYS. (B = Beverley.)

(MS. of date 1430–1440; in possession of the Earl of
Ashburnham.)

1–6. Creation. Fall of Lucifer. Adam and Eve. Garden
of Eden. Man's Disobedience and Fall. (B. Five
plays.)

7. Sacrificium Cayne et Abell. (B.)

8–9. Building of the Ark. Noah and his Wife and the
Flood. (B.)

10. Abraham's Sacrifice. (B.)

11. Departure of Israelites from Egypt. The Ten Plagues
and Passage of Red Sea.

12. Prologue of Prophets.   Annunciation and Visit to Eliza-
      beth.   (B.)

13. Joseph's Trouble about Mary.

14. Journey to Jerusalem.   Birth of Jesus.   (B.)

15. The Angels and Shepherds.   (B.)

16–17. Coming of the Three Kings to Herod.   Adoration.   (B.)

18. Flight into Egypt.   (B.)

19. Massacre of the Innocents.   (B.)

20. Christ with the Doctors in the Temple.   (B.)

21. Baptism of Jesus.   (B.)

22. The Temptation.   (B.)

23. The Transfiguration.

24. Woman taken in Adultery.   Lazarus.   (B.)

25. Entry into Jerusalem.   (B.)   The Blind.   The Lame.
      Zaccheus.

26. Conspiracy to take Jesus.

27. The Last Supper.   (B.)

28. The Agony and Betrayal.   (B.)

29. Peter's Denial.   Jesus before Caiphas.   (B.)

30. Dream of Pilate's Wife.   (B.)

31–33. Trials before Herod (B.) and Pilate (B.).   Remorse of
      Judas.

34. Christ led up to Calvary.

35. Crucifixion.

36. Mortificatio.   (B.)   Burial of Jesus.

37. Harrowing of Hell.   (B.)

38. Resurrection.   (B.)   The Three Marys.

39. Christ appears to Mary Magdalene.

40. Travellers to Emmaus.   (B.)

41. Purification.   (B.)

42. Incredulity of Thomas.

43. Ascension.   (B.)

44. Descent of the Holy Spirit.

45. Death of Mary.

46. Appearance of Mary to Thomas.

47. Assumption and Coronation (B.) of Virgin.
48. The Judgment Day. (B.)

NOTE. — The Beverley series was originally a cycle of 36 plays, closely correspondent to the York cycle. Titles only are extant.

See

Smith, Lucy Toulmin. York Plays. 1885. Full Cycle.

Collier, J. P. Camden Miscellany. Vol. IV. 1859.
     Play Forty-second. Incredulity of St. Thomas.

Croft, J. Excerpta Antiqua. 1797.
     Play Forty-second. Incredulity of St. Thomas.

Pollard, A. W. English Miracle Plays, Moralities and Interludes.
     Play First: The Creation and the Fall of Lucifer.

See also

Anglia X. '87–'88.
     Die Quellen der York Spiele.
     (Leipziger Dissertation. 1887. P. Kamann.)

Anglia XI. '88–'89.
     Die Altenglischen Kollektivmisterien.
     Unter besonderer Berücksichtigung des Verhältnisses der York und Towneley Spiele. Alex. Holdfeld.

Herltrich, O. Studien zu den York Plays. Breslau. 1886.
     (Dissertation.)

See for parallel reading

Cursor Mundi. Edited by Richard Morris. 1874. (E. E. T. S.)

b. Towneley Plays.

     (Also known as Widkirk, Woodkirk, Wakefield. MS. of fifteenth century, in possession of B. Quaritch, 15 Piccadilly, London.)

1. Creatio.
2. Mactatio Abel.
3. Processus Noe cum Filiis.
4. Abraham.

5. Isaac.
6. Jacob.
7. Processus Prophetarum.
8. Pharao.
9. Cæsar Augustus.
10. Annunciatio.
11. Salutacio Elizabeth.
12. Prima Pagina Pastorum.
13. Secunda Pagina Pastorum.
14. Oblacio Magorum.
15. Fugacio in Ægyptum.
16. Magnus Herodus.
17. Purificacio Mariæ.
18. Pagina Doctorum.
19. Johannes Babtista.
20. Conspiracio et Capcio.
21. Coliphizatio.
22. Flagellacio.
23. Processus Crucis. Crucifixio.
24. Processus Talentorum.
25. Extractio Animarum ab Inferno.
26. Resurrectio Domini.
27. Peregrini.
28. Thomas Indiæ.
29. Ascencio Domini.
30. Juditium.
31. Lazarus.
32. Suspentio Judæ.

See

Stevenson, J. S. Towneley Mysteries. Edited for the Surtees Society. 1836. Full Cycle.

Marriott, William. Collection of English Miracle Plays. 1838.
Play Eighth. Pharao.
Play Thirteenth. Pastores.
Play Twenty-third. Crucifixio.

Play Twenty-fifth.   Extractio Animarum ab Inferno.

Play Thirtieth.   Juditium.

Collier, J. P.   Five Miracle Plays or Scriptural Dramas.   1836.

Play Thirteenth.   Secunda Pagina Pastorum.

Pollard, A. W.   English Miracle Plays, Moralities and Interludes.

Play Thirteenth.   Secunda Pastorum (abridged).

Douce, F.   Roxburghe Club Publications.   No. 16.

Play Thirtieth.   Juditium.

NOTE.—A new edition of the Towneley Plays, greatly needed, will shortly be issued by the Early English Text Society.

c. CHESTER PLAYS.

(Five MSS. of dates 1591–1607, three in British Museum, one in Bodleian, one in possession of the Duke of Devonshire.)

Banes or Prologue.

1. The Fall of Lucifer.
2. The Creation and Fall, and Death of Abel.
3. Noah's Flood.
4. The Histories of Lot and Abraham.
5. Balaam and his Ass.
6. The Salutation ·and Nativity (with prophecies from Octavian and the Sibyl).
7. The Play of the Shepherds.
8. The Three Kings come to Herod.
9. Offering of the Three Kings.
10. Slaughter of the Innocents.
11. The Purification.
12. The Temptation, and the Woman taken in Adultery.
13. (Cure of the Blind Man.)   Lazarus.
14. Christ's Entry into Jerusalem.
15. Christ's Betrayal.
16. The Passion.
17. The Crucifixion.

18. The Harrowing of Hell.
19. The Resurrection (and the Three Marys).
20. The Pilgrims of Emaus.
21. The Ascension.
22. The Emission of the Holy Ghost.
23. Ezechiel (Prophesies of the End of the World and Fifteen Signs of Doom).
24. Antichrist.
25. Doomsday.

See

Wright, Thomas. Chester Mysteries. Edited for the Shakespeare Society. 1843–1847. Full Cycle.

Deimling, Hermann. The Chester Plays. Part I. 1892. (Part II. in preparation.) Full Cycle. E. E. T. S.

Markland, J. H. Roxburghe Club Publications. No. 11. 1818. Banes or Prologue.
Play Third. De Deluvio Noe.
Play Tenth. De Occisione Innocentium.

Marriott, William. Collection of English Miracle Plays. 1838.
Play Third. The Deluge.
Play Twenty-fourth. Antichrist.

Collier, J. P. Five Miracle Plays or Scriptural Dramas. 1836.
Play Twenty-fourth. Antichrist.

Pollard, A. W. English Miracle Plays, Moralities and Interludes.
Play Third. Noah's Flood.
Play Fourth. (Portion) The Sacrifice of Isaac.

   d. COVENTRY PLAYS.

         (MS. of date 1534, burned in 1879 at Birmingham.)

Prologue.
1. Creation.
2. Fall of Man.
3. Cain and Abel.
4. Noah's Flood. (Lamack kills Cain.)
5. Abraham's Sacrifice.

6. Moses and the Two Tables.
7. The Prophets.
8. The Barrenness of Anna.
9. Mary in the Temple.
10. Mary's Betrothment.
11. The Salutation and Conception.
12. Joseph's Return.
13. The Visit to Elizabeth.
14. The Trial of Joseph and Mary.
15. Birth of Christ.
16. Adoration of the Shepherds.
17. Adoration of the Magi.
18. The Purification.
19. Slaughter of the Innocents.
20. Christ disputing in the Temple.
21. The Baptism of Christ.
22. The Temptation.
23. The Woman taken in Adultery.
24. Lazarus.
25. The Council of the Jews.
26. Entry into Jerusalem.
27. The Last Supper.
28. Betraying of Christ.
29. King Herod.
30. Trial of Christ.
31. Pilate's Wife's Dream.
32. Condemnation and Crucifixion of Christ.
33. The Descent into Hell.
34. Burial of Christ.
35. Resurrection (and part of Descent).
36. The Three Marys.
37. Christ appearing to Mary.
38. Pilgrim of Emaus (and Incredulity of Thomas).
39. Ascension.
40. Descent of the Holy Ghost.

41. Assumption of the Virgin.
42. Domesday.
See

Halliwell, J. O.   Ludus Coventriæ.   Edited for the Shakespeare
Society.   1841.   Full Cycle.

Marriott, William.   Collection of English Miracle Plays.   1838.
Play Twelfth.   Joseph's Jealousy.
Play Fourteenth.   The Trial of Mary and Joseph.

Collier, J. P.   Five Miracle Plays or Scriptural Dramas.   1836.
Play Tenth.   Marriage of the Virgin.

Pollard, A. W.   English Miracle Plays, Moralities and Inter-
ludes.
Play Eleventh.   The Salutation and Conception.
See also

Sharp, Thomas.   Dissertation on the Pageants or Dramatic
Mysteries anciently performed at Coventry.   1825.

NOTE.— Sharp has printed privately the Coventry guild pageant of the
Shearmen and Taylors, viz., The Nativity, and for the Abbotsford Club the
guild pageant of the Weavers, viz., The Presentation in the Temple and
Disputation with the Doctors.

e. CORNWALL PLAYS.

(MS. of 14th Century in Cornish, in possession of
Bodleian Library.)

1. Origo Mundi.
2. Passio Domini Nostri.
3. Resurrexio Domini Nostri.
See

Norris, Edwin.   Origo Mundi; Passio Domini Nostri: Resurrexio Domini Nostri.   Ancient Cornish Drama; edited and
translated.   1859.
See for parallel reading

Stokes, Whitley.   The Passion.   Philological Society Transactions.   1860–61.   Appendix.

f. DUBLIN PLAYS.

> (Date of MS. 1420–1450, Trinity College, Dublin.)

Abraham and Isaac.

See

Collier, J. P.   Five Miracle Plays or Scriptural Dramas.   1836.

g. PLAYS OF NEWCASTLE-ON-TYNE.

> (MS. at Newcastle.)

Noah's Ark.

See

Sharp, Thomas.   Dissertation on the Pageants or Dramatic Mysteries anciently performed at Coventry.   1825.

NOTE. — This play is also printed in two histories of Newcastle, one by Henry Bourne, 1736, the other by John Brand, 1789.

II. Isolated Plays.

a. NORFOLK.

> (MS. of fifteenth century at Brome Hall, Suffolk County.)

1. Abraham and Isaac.

See

Rye, Walter.   Norfolk Antiquarian Miscellany.   Vol. III., Part I.

Smith, Lucy Toulmin.   The Book of Brome.

Smith, Lucy Toulmin.   Anglia.   VII.

Pollard, A. W.   English Miracle Plays, Moralities and Interludes.   Appendix.

2. The Play of the Sacrament.

> (MS. of date about 1461.   Trinity College, Dublin.)

See

Stokes, Whitley.   Philological Society Transactions.   1860–61. Appendix.

b. NORWICH.

> (Two MSS. 1534 and 1565, in possession of Robert Fitch, Norwich.)

1. The Story of the Creaĉon of Eve, with the Expyllng of Adam and Eve out of Paradyce.   The Grocers' Play.

NOTE. — This play was privately printed by Robert Fitch in 1856.   See also Norfolk and Norwich Archæological Society Proceedings.   Vol. III.

c. DIGBY.

(Digby MS. of late fifteenth century, Bodleian Library.)
1. The Killing of the Children.
2. Conversion of Saint Paul.
3. Mary Magdalene.
    (MS. of early sixteenth century, Bodleian Library.)
4. Burial and Resurrection of Christ.
See

Furnivall, F. J.   Digby Mysteries.   Edited for the New Shakspere Society.   1882.

Sharp, Thomas.   Ancient Mysteries from the Digby Manuscripts.   1835.
    The Killing of the Children.
    Conversion of Saint Paul.
    Mary Magdalene.

Hawkins, Thomas.   Origin of the English Drama.   1773.
    The Killing of the Children : Parfre's Candlemas Day.

Marriott, William.   A Collection of English Miracle Plays.
    The Killing of the Children of Israel, or Candlemas Day.

Pollard, A. W.   English Miracle Plays, Moralities and Interludes.
    Mary Magdalene.   (Portion.)

Halliwell, J. O.   Reliquiæ Antiquæ.   1843.
    Christ's Burial and Resurrection.
    See also

Schmidt, K.   Die Digby-Spiele.   1884.   Berlin.   (Dissertation.)

d. CORNISH.

(MS. of date 1611 in Cornish, Bodleian Library.)
1. The Creation of the World, with Noah's Flood.

(MS. of date 1504 in Cornish, in possession of Sir Watkins Williams Winn, Hengwyrt Collection, Peniarth, Wales.)

2. Life of Saint Meriasek.

See

Gilbert, Davies. The Creation of the World, with Noah's Flood.
    Edited 1827. (With English translation by John Keigwin.)
Stokes. Whitley. Life of Saint Meriasek. Edited and translated 1872.

NOTE.— With the foregoing should be compared the dramatic poem, *Harrowing of Hell*, printed by Collier in his Five Miracle Plays and privately printed by Halliwell. Of the Protestant Mysteries of Bishop Bale (1495–1563) four are extant. *The Three Laws of Nature, Moses and Christ* remains in manuscript. *God's Promises* is printed in the first volume of Dodsley's Old Plays, and by Marriott in his collection of English Miracle Plays. *The Temptacyon of Our Lord* has been edited by Grosart among the Miscellanies of the Fuller Worthies' Library, Vol. I., and the *Johan Baptystes preachynge in the Wildernesse* is printed in the first volume of the Harleian Miscellany. There exist a few other Biblical dramas, late and inferior, as *Jacob and Esau, Pharaoh's Daughter, Joseph and his Brothers*, but these have no place in a consideration of genuine Miracle Plays. See also Stephen's Dictionary of National Biography for account of a Latin Miracle by John Foxe the Martyrologist.

Summary of English Miracle Plays.

CYCLES.

London.
Worcester. } Plays entirely lost.
Beverley.

	Original Number.	Extant.
York	48	48
Towneley	32	32
Chester	25	25
Coventry	42	42
Cornwall	3	3
Dublin	14	1
Newcastle-on-Tyne	16	1

152

ISOLATED PLAYS.

		Extant.
Norfolk	. . . .	2
Norwich	. . . .	1
Digby	. . . .	4
Cornish	. . . .	2
	Total of Extant Plays	161

C. ENGLISH MORALITIES.

I. Full Scope Moralities.   (Fifteenth Century.)

The Macro Moralities.

  The Castell of Perseverance.

  Mind, Will, and Understanding.

  Mankind.

Mundus et Infans.

The Pride of Life.   (Fragment.)

Everyman.

Nature.   By Henry Medwall.

II. Limited Moralities.

  a. DEALING WITH TEMPTATIONS OF YOUTH.

Hycke-Scorner.   Printed about 1530.

Lusty Juventus.   1547–1553.

The Interlude of Youth.   1553–1558.

  b. WRITTEN IN PRAISE OF LEARNING.

The Nature of the Four Elements.   1510–1520.

Wyt and Science.   By Jhon Redford.   About 1545.

III. Transitional Moralities.

  a. WRITTEN BY PROFESSIONAL POETS.

Magnyfycence.   By John Skelton.   1515–1523.

Ane Satyre of the Thrie Estaitis.   By Sir David Lyndsay.

  1535–1540.

b. APPEARED IN SHAKESPEARE'S BOYHOOD.

The longer Thou livest the more Foole Thou art. By W. Wager. Early Elizabethan.

Triall of Treasure. Printed 1567. (Two editions.)

Like wil to like quod the Devel to the Colier. By Ulpian Fulwel. Printed 1568.

The Marriage of Witte and Science. (Adapted from Redford's Wyt and Science.) Licensed 1569–1570.

New Custome. Printed 1573.

The Tyde taryeth no Man. By George Wapull. Printed 1576.

All for Money. By T. Lupton. Printed 1578.

The Marriage between Witt and Wisdome. 1579.

The Three Ladies of London. 1584.

c. BELATED.

The Three Lords and Three Ladies of London. 1590.

The Contention between Liberality and Prodigality. 1602.

Microcosmus. By Thomas Nabbes. 1637.

NOTE. — Portions of *The Castell of Perseverance* are printed in Pollard's English Miracle Plays. A portion of *Mind, Will and Understanding*, under title of *A Morality of Wisdom Who is Christ*, is printed in Furnivall's Digby Mysteries. *The Macro Moralities* are soon to be edited by Pollard for the E. E. T. S. *Mundus et Infans* was printed by Wynkyn de Worde, 1522, a reprint being issued by the Roxburghe Club in 1817. This Morality is easily accessible in the twelfth volume of Dodsley's Old Plays. *Everyman* was printed four times early in the sixteenth century, twice by Richard Pynson and twice by John Skot. It is accessible in the first volume of Hawkins' Origin of the English Drama, in Hazlitt's Dodsley, Vol. I., and, in abridged form, in Pollard's English Miracle Plays. *Nature* survives in printed form, but without date or printer's name. Of the later Moralities, *Hycke-Scorner* is accessible in Hawkins' Origin of the English Drama, Vol. I., and in Hazlitt's Dodsley, Vol. I.; *Lusty Juventus*, in Hawkins' Origin of the English Drama, Vol. I., and in Dodsley's Old Plays, Vol. II.; *The Interlude of Youth*, in Hazlitt's Dodsley, Vol. II.; *The Nature of the Four Elements*, in Hazlitt's Dodsley, Vol. I., in Percy Society Publications, Vol. XXIII., and in Pollard's Miracle Plays; *Wyt and Science*, in the Shakespeare Society Publications for 1848 (edited by Halliwell); *Magnyfycence*, in Dyce's edition of Skelton's Poetical Works; *Ane Satyre of the*

Thrie Estaitis, in Laing's edition of Lyndsay's Poetical Works; *Triall of Treasure*, in Hazlitt's Dodsley, Vol. III., and in Percy Society Publications, Vol. XXVIII. (edited by Halliwell); *Like wil to Like*, in Hazlitt's Dodsley, Vol. III.; *The Marriage of Witte and Science*, in Hazlitt's Dodsley, Vol. II.; *New Custome*, in Hazlitt's Dodsley, Vol. III.; *The Tyde Taryeth no Man*, in Collier's Illustrations of Early English Literature, 1863, Vol. II.; *The Marriage between Witt and Wisdome*, in the Shakespeare Society Publications for 1846; *The Three Ladies of London* and *The Three Lords and Three Ladies of London*, in Hazlitt's Dodsley, Vol. VI.; *The Contention between Liberality and Prodigality*, in Hazlitt's Dodsley, Vol. VIII.; and *Microcosmus*, in Hazlitt's Dodsley, Vol. IX. See also Shakespeare Society Publications, 1844, for *Albyon Knight*, fragment of a political Morality.

IV. Early Comedies with Morality Features.

> *e.g.*, Jack Juggler. About 1560.
>> The Disobedient Child. By Th. Ingelend. Printed in 1560.
>> Common Conditions. About 1570.
>> Gammer Gurton's Needle. Perhaps by John Still. Before 1575.
>> Tom Tiler and his Wife. 1578.

V. Early Tragedies with Morality Features.

> *e.g.*, Bishop Bale's Kynge Johan. About 1550.
> The Nice Wanton. 1560.
> Cambises. About 1561.
> Apius and Virginia. About 1563.
> The Conflict of Conscience. 1581.

NOTE. — Of these later plays, *Jack Juggler* is printed in Hazlitt's Dodsley, Vol. II., and in Child's Four Old Plays; *The Disobedient Child*, in Hazlitt's Dodsley, Vol. II., and in Percy Society Publications, Vol. XXIII.; *Gammer Gurton's Needle*, in Dodsley's Old Plays, Vol. II., in Hazlitt's Dodsley, Vol. III., in The Ancient British Drama, Vol. I., and in Hawkins' Origin of the English Drama; Bale's *Kynge Johan*, in the Camden Society's Publications, 1838, and Pollard's English Miracle Plays; *The Nice Wanton*, in Hazlitt's Dodsley, Vol. II.; *Cambises*, in Hawkins' Origin of the English Drama, Vol. I., and Hazlitt's Dodsley, Vol. IV.; *Apius and Virginia*, in Dodsley's Old Plays, Vol. XII.; *The Conflict of Conscience*, in the Roxburghe Club Publications for 1851, and Hazlitt's Dodsley, Vol. VI.